The Sacred Science of Yoga &
The Five Koshas

Christopher Sartain

DEDICATION

I dedicate this book to all my teachers, especially the teachers of the
Kriya Yoga lineage of Masters; Mahavatar Babaji, Lahiri Mahasaya,
Sri Yukteswar, Paramahansa Yogananda, and Roy Eugene Davis and
their successors.

CONTENTS

Acknowledgments i

1 Identity Crisis 1

2 The Witness 9

3 The Five Koshas 21

4 Annamaya Kosha 27

5 Pranamaya Kosha 39

6 Manamaya Kosha 51

7 Vijnanamaya Kosha 59

8 Anandamaya Kosha 65

9 Experiences with a Master 69

10 Ecstatic Poems 81

ACKNOWLEDGMENTS

I acknowledge the constant inspiration of the Sangre de Cristo mountain range with all its uplifting energy. The magnificent natural beauty around my home was a major contributing factor in the completion of this work. I would also like to thank and acknowledge the love and support of my family, and especially my wife, Carolina.

1 IDENTITY CRISIS

Most human suffering comes about as a result of a mistaken sense of self-identity. One suffers because they believe they are something they are not. The materialists and scientists of our age have permeated our mainstream culture with the ideas that we are nothing more than flesh and bone. A freak accident in the random affairs of evolution...a physical being, and nothing more. Most scientists would have us believe that we are an amalgamation of organic molecules and that when our body dies and these organic molecules cease to function properly, our entire Being is forever erased.

The great Spiritual Masters throughout the ages have taught that we are not just what we see reflected in the mirror. The enlightened teachers from all ages and cultures have taught us that we are much more than just our physical body and that our Being is composed of multiple layers or dimensions. We possess as human beings the potential to have experiences outside of the known physical layer of reality. Although these experiences are not always easy to prove, there is a mounting preponderance of evidence that we do in fact have an astral or energetic body, and furthermore that all humans are interconnected in a complex field of Consciousness outside the bounds of space-time.

As the human race begins to Awaken to the truth of its Spiritual existence many people will have a difficult time letting go of their traditional religious dogmas and they will require qualified guides to lead them to the Truth. The great Yogi Paramahansa Yogananda once told my Spiritual Teacher Roy Eugene Davis, "...in the future there will be many souls seeking God and there won't be enough qualified teachers to teach them..." I believe we have reached such a time. It is of the utmost importance that people begin to take their personal Awakening seriously and that they pass on what they have learned to souls yearning for truth, knowledge, and wisdom.

It will be increasingly implausible in the coming years for people to cling to antiquated belief systems that no longer serve humanity and planet Earth. It is essential for people to acknowledge their Infinity in order to end collective human suffering. If we continue to act out of "personality consciousness" then we can expect a continuation of many of the problems facing humanity. It is time we Awaken to our fullest human potential and realize once and for all that we are all part of God and that we are experiencing eternal life currently. There is no need to wait for a future heaven to experience eternal life...we are Infinite in the Here and Now!

When one is able to calm their mind and sit in the stillness of their Being, there is still a sense that "I am". It is this "I am-ness" that is our true, Infinite nature. Behind the facade of the personality is our higher Self. The practice of meditation allows us to experience our higher Self and move beyond the denser layers of our Being. Most people, upon realizing that they are not who they thought they were, have a difficult time accepting the true nature of their existence. I think the vast majority of seekers experience some degree of discomfort upon learning that they are not their name, likes, and dislikes, family, looks, personality, etc... Personality is merely a shell that allows us to grow inside Spiritually while executing our roles and karmic duties here on Earth. It is temporary and has no real permanent existence. Therefore, by believing that we are our personalities and physical bodies, we enter into a delusional state that, in 99.999% of humans, lasts an entire lifetime. The vast majority of humans never Awaken from personality-consciousness and they die thinking that they will either no longer exist, or that their personality-self will go to Heaven to live with Jesus or another hero character from the distant past.

In reality, when we die, our Consciousness migrates with our astral body to the astral plane and then delivers it into another form until that form dies, and the process continues indefinitely as we evolve and Awaken to our true nature. Reincarnation is the process of birth, death, and rebirth that humans cycle through as they move towards Oneness and Enlightenment. If one believes that they only live for but one brief lifetime, then their suffering is exacerbated by an underlying anxiety that at some point they will simply cease to exist. This fear of death is paralyzing and is one of the greatest obstacles preventing our Spiritual growth and development.

Nothing ever happens to the "real" us. At our core, we are Infinite and remain unaffected in every situation, even death. There is no need to fear anything because we are Infinite. We cannot die. It is simply impossible for us to cease to exist. We have always existed and we will never stop existing. The death of the body is but a transition from one lifetime to the next. There is no need to dread the death of the body and personality. When this body dies, our astral body carries our Consciousness with it to the astral plane and when it is time the astral body becomes involved with another form based upon its karma and the law of attraction, and the process starts all over again.

When we identify with the temporary self, we suffer. When we learn to transcend the finite body-mind-personality complex and bring our awareness in line with our Infinite Self, we end our suffering. The process by which one may move their awareness through the various layers of their Being until they reach their Infinite core is known as Yoga. Yoga is an ancient system of actions meant to arouse in the practitioner an experience of their highest Self, leaving a lasting imprint or residue that returns the practitioner's Consciousness back to its original wholeness.

Suffering has always been mistakenly assumed to be a "bad" thing. Suffering is, in fact, a great gift. Without suffering it is impossible to react, adapt, and evolve. In a state of nature, all animals must be confronted by obstacles and changes in their environments that force them to react, adapt, and evolve. Suffering is the food of Spiritual evolution. Suffering is what feeds the fires of our growth and development. Without it, we would never move around or attempt to better our lives or situations. Just as a plant grows towards the light around any obstacles that might get in its way, so too does our soul grow towards the Light of God around whatever obstacles and suffering that might confront it.

Without suffering how would the soul know non-suffering? It would have no basis for comparison. Suffering allows Consciousness to move ever closer to perfection because Consciousness begins to find ways around suffering just as a plant begins to find ways around obstacles to find the light of the sun. Without the obstacles, how would the plant know where to go? Suffering gives us direction and shows us where we need to grow and develop so that we may reach maturation. Without it, we would have no direction, no focus, nowhere to go, nothing to do. However, there are those fortunate few who have overcome their suffering, and these Masters have found that the only thing left to do once their own suffering is vanquished is to teach others how to end suffering. In Buddhism, there is a term for such teachers; they are known as bodhisattvas. These are saintly individuals who have transcended all suffering and have made it their most sacred vow to end suffering in all sentient beings.

We can see from the fossil record that some species such as the Coelacanth have not changed much at all for millions of years. For instance, the Coelacanth has supposedly existed for three hundred and ninety million years now unchanged. This is because their habitat has not changed for millions of years either. They have not had to respond to any changing stimuli that would lead to further complexity so they have stayed relatively simple. The same cannot be said for humans and most other species on planet Earth. It looks like humans most likely had to respond to a constantly changing environment in their storied past and to a great degree still do today. Ancient humans no doubt suffered far more than we do today with our modernized technological society with every possible comfort available to us...in some countries anyway. It was the suffering of ancient man that led to his evolution and intelligence and it is the suffering of man that has brought about every great revolution and innovation in human history.

Each time we suffer, we should embrace it as an opportunity for healing, growth, and evolution. Every time we get angry, afraid, jealous, sad, or anxious we are confronted with a wonderful chance to overcome and to heal. Suffering is often times what brings people to Spirituality in the first place. Many Masters have said that people come to the path in one of two ways; either through an intense longing for God, or through intense suffering. And in reality, maybe sometimes it's a little bit of both, as was my case looking back now. But the point is that many people do come to meditation and other practices as a way to escape their suffering, which is perfectly fine. Spirituality, of course, should not be viewed as escapism, but we cannot ignore the beneficial role that suffering plays in bringing many souls to God. When one attempts to find ways around their suffering, they are establishing a Spiritual practice whether they know it or not. Because we do not possess near the number of qualified teachers and Masters on planet Earth at this time, many people seek to escape their suffering through temporary material means such as alcohol and television. If we had more Spiritual teachers around, then perhaps more people would be educated about the inadequacy of the finite to satisfy the Infinite. Physical things come and go; your everlasting soul is forever.

At our core, we are all-knowing and Infinite. Everything is available to us in Reality. There are no limits or boundaries. Any boundary or limit is an illusion of the human mind. Even the perceived difference between an immoral criminal and an enlightened Master is just an illusion. Our true nature, what the Buddhists call Buddha nature, is all knowing. There is no limit to what we can know and discover. Layer by layer, our illusory self fades away and we realize that we are Infinite and have limitless potential. I have seen miraculous events in my own lifetime and so have millions of others. I have heard stories from my Spiritual Teacher, Roy Eugene Davis, that are mesmerizing and difficult to believe at first, until you begin to see things in your own life that validate what you have read in books and heard from Masters.

Suffering is a necessary component for Spiritual growth and evolution. Without it, we would be like the Coelacanth, unchanged for three hundred and ninety million years. Souls incarnate here on Earth to suffer. That is why they keep coming back. Souls are attracted back to bodies on planet Earth to come here and suffer so that they may learn, grow, and evolve towards perfection. We cannot eliminate karma without suffering. The Spiritual path is the process of eliminating karma and growing towards the Light, but the Spiritual

5

path cannot exist without karma, without obstacles, without suffering. We would not know what the Light looked like without the darkness.

Our shadows are what propel us forward and allow us to bend and move and grow towards the Light of God. Our shadows are our greatest teachers. But our shadows are not who we are. They too are impermanent and cannot cause any lasting suffering and are not to be feared. We are not our shadows, suffering, or our karma; they are temporary and can be transcended. They are but our teachers and are to be embraced and accepted as part of the process and part of the path to Light.

The idea that one is their personality and that they can only experience eternal life by accepting an ancient hero figure unsubstantiated by history is a fiction. We are living an eternal life in the Here and Now. There is no need to wait. It is happening as you read this page. We are not our body because it changes, we are not our emotions because they change, we are not our memories because they change, we are not our desires because they change, we are not our karma because it changes, we are not our thoughts because they change, we are not our family because it changes, we are not our likes and dislikes because they change. We are none of these things. We are instead that which never changes. We are that which rests in the stillness of the eternal abyss of peace and balance and observes all of the changing tides of this illusion. We are unbounded Infinite Consciousness, or what many have termed, the Witness.

To end human suffering it is essential for us to sever our identification with our temporary self that has no fixed reality and instead begin to identify with a larger sense of Self; a sense of Self that encompasses everything and everyone. In doing so, not only does one end their own suffering, but they also realize that they are One with everything and everyone. Once a person experiences the wholeness of the universe in their Being and realizes that they are essentially the exact same thing as everyone else, violence towards another human being is impossible. The realization of one's true nature brings about a sense of compassion and love for everything and everyone. As more people begin to Awaken to their true nature, global peace will finally become a real possibility. Roy Eugene Davis has said, "when one person wakes up, it makes the collective Consciousness just a little bit brighter and that benefits all sentient beings since we're all connected."

2 THE WITNESS

When the mind is still and quiet, it is possible to experience oneself as the observer or Witness. Thoughts float by on the screen of one's Consciousness without any resulting reaction or vibration. During deep meditation, one can experience the changing, undulating nature of their mind and physical being and merge the awareness with that which does not change; Unbounded Infinite Consciousness. The resulting calmness that occurs upon learning that one can simply witness any disturbances or emotional reactions in their bodies without identifying with them is liberating in and of itself.

It is easy to get a taste of the Witness by sitting still in an upright position and removing awareness from all mental noise. We can begin to notice thoughts rising and falling, but without any reaction. It is often times helpful to pretend as though we are viewing someone else's thoughts during this practice. This type of disassociation from our thoughts makes us less likely to want to identify with them and allows us to remain more objective. We can watch the movements of the mind as though we were watching the movements of someone else's mind without any attachment to the contents of the movements.

When a thought arises we observe the thought with dispassionate objectivity until the thought fades and we rest in the silence...then another thought arises and we watch it without reaction until it fades, and so on and so forth. This is the best training I've found for merging our awareness with the Witness. As we continue to practice in this way, we can eventually begin to experience thought-free states where we are fully at one with Witness Consciousness. Over time, as we merge our awareness more and more with the objective observer, we can start to get a glimpse of our true nature.

To understand the Witness is to understand that suffering is impossible in ultimate Reality. If one truly believes that they are, at their core, the Witness or Pure Consciousness then one must also believe that they cannot suffer at their core since the Witness always remains unaffected. Suffering is an illusion of the mind. In the deepest layers of ultimate Reality, suffering does not occur. Therefore, to end suffering we must align or merge our attention and awareness with our true Infinite nature that is always serene, peaceful, and enlightened.

Daily mediation practice is the easiest way to repeatedly merge the awareness with the Witness. While there are those few blessed individuals who have suddenly awoken without the use of meditation, or mind-altering practices, it is rare. Most people require a consistent daily practice of bringing their attention into alignment with Infinite Consciousness until it becomes more permanent. Most of the great Masters throughout the ages have recommended a daily meditation practice as the most efficient path to Spiritual growth. There is no safer and more effective way to see one's true nature than to sit in the stillness of pure Being on a daily basis.

The Witness, Infinite Consciousness, God, or whatever one chooses to call it, is indefinable. All physical manifestation vibrates at a certain frequency no matter how small or subtle, whether we are talking about quarks and subatomic particles or thoughts. However, all vibration and physicality comes from a place of no vibration. There is a substratum underlying all of creation that has no vibratory frequency and that never changes. In order for something to change, it must vibrate. In order for something to vibrate, it must change. The Witness does not change. It is like a perfectly still lake with no ripples or waves. As soon as a thought occurs in the mind, a ripple is created and a resulting thought-form bursts into manifestation creating a vibratory frequency that can even be measured now by science. Thought-forms may also be felt by people in a room. For instance, I think we have all had the experience of having someone walk into a room with negative energy and then experiencing a sudden change of mood. One need not have psychic powers to feel the energy associated with thoughts, both negative and positive.

Unbounded Infinite Consciousness is how Patanjali describes our highest nature in his bible of Yoga, the Yoga Sutras. But even this does not entirely convey to a seeker the sheer magnitude of ultimate Reality. Our mind is finite and therefore can only think in finite terms. For us to understand something that is unbounded or Infinite is impossible. Our minds simply cannot comprehend that which is beyond the finite. Therefore, it is of little use to attempt to describe the Witness or our highest nature. To try and do so in the company of a Zen Buddhist for example would be sacrilege. The Zen tradition realizes that the highest truth cannot be conveyed via words or language. A word is just a cognitive label we use to have some understanding of our environment so that we may organize our thoughts into coherent and logical patterns so we can function here on planet Earth. But words do not express the reality of an object. A tree is not the word tree. The word merely describes the object, but it can never convey the reality or essence of a tree. If words cannot do a tree justice, then they have no business attempting to describe God.

The best way to understand that which cannot be understood is to **experience** it firsthand in your Being. Rather than just believing what might have been read in a text or heard in a discourse, it is far superior to know. Roy Eugene Davis has always said, "Don't be a believer...be a knower!" Within us already lies all knowledge. We have everything we need within our Being. There is no need for us to have faith in what others have said or written. We can know what they know. To believe in something is to imply that there exists some amount of doubt, but to know something erases all doubt. Furthermore, experiential knowledge that arises from deep within our Being is superior to knowledge gained in books or lectures.

In Patanjali's Yoga Sutras, Patanjali states that the knowledge gained through direct experience is qualitatively different than knowledge gained from book learning. I can attest to this, as I have had some direct experience of the Divine Oneness and I can say without any doubt that the knowledge gained through meditation and direct experience is qualitatively different than any knowledge I have ever gained by reading something or attending a lecture. This type of knowledge cannot be measured quantitatively. It is therefore said to differ qualitatively since quality cannot be measured objectively. I cannot say for sure that the knowledge that I gained through superconscious states is measurably different from knowledge gained through other means, but I can say for sure that the **quality** of the knowledge is far greater than that gained through other means.

In 2011 I was attending a six day Rounding retreat in the North Georgia Mountains where I was living at the time. Rounding is a Yogic technique for awakening Kundalini (potential energy) and having Samadhi experiences. One Round consists of 20 minutes Yoga Asana, 10 minute Savasana, 5 minutes of Pranayama, 20 minutes of meditation, 10 minute Savasana, and 5 minutes of Sanskrit chanting. One then takes a 15 minute break and does another Round. We were doing five or six of these Rounds a day for six days in a row. This is the most powerful Spiritual technique I've come across and is the true Raja Yoga or "Royal Path" Yoga, which engages and purifies every layer of our Being.

On the fifth day of the retreat, following the second round I experienced what I can only call a full Awakening experience. Right after we finished the chanting, my identification with Christopher Sartain vanished. I was no longer identified with my finite self, but was instead identified with a much larger sense of Self. I laid down on the floor and was overwhelmed by waves of bliss energy flowing through my body. I could feel the nectar of the Lord caressing every dimension of my Being. It was like nothing I had ever experienced up to that point, and to be honest, I haven't had an experience quite that powerful since. Bathed in bliss, I can faintly remember hearing voices as others were leaving the room and heading to the dining hall for lunch.

I heard the voices, but I wasn't separate from them. I was them. Christopher was not the one hearing the voices or experiencing the voices. The sounds were no longer happening around me, but in me. I was that. I was everything. I was a singular point of Consciousness expanding in every direction and able to "see" in my third eye three hundred and sixty degrees around me. It was like matter became aware of Spirit and Spirit became aware of matter and they realized simultaneously that they were One.

After what felt like about thirty minutes, I was able to stand up and walk outside. When I first stood up, my spine began shaking uncontrollably, but calmed down after a few minutes. I wandered into the woods, took off all my clothing and sat down and stared at a tree for about one hour. I was still in a thought-free state of Oneness. There was only the Witness. My attention and awareness was entirely merged with the observer...fully present. I stood up again, and walked to an overlook of the North Georgia mountains where the retreat was. I sat and stared at mountains for about another thirty minutes or so completely identified with the Oneness of the Lord. Spirit and Matter, Shiva and Shakti, Yin and Yang were married alchemically in my Being and I was forever changed.

I finally came back to "normalcy" when I began having a few thoughts. I wanted to share what I was experiencing with the others at the retreat. I was so excited and thrilled that I wanted to stand up and share my experience and the energy in my Being with others. Then I had the thought, "What would they think?" "How would they react?" Then it was over...ego had crept back in and I was worried again about how the other would view the Christopher Sartain character. The experience was over, but when one has a breakthrough like that, there is a residue that stays with them forever.

It is this residue that ought to be the aim of any serious Yoga and meditation practice. Otherwise, Yoga is just stretching and breathing and meditation is just sitting in one place for a while. Yoga and meditation are ancient practices handed down to us by Masters from bygone ages and these practices should be taken seriously and treated with respect. There is nothing wrong with using these practices for stress reduction or their overall health benefits, but any serious practitioner must know that the end result of a consistent Spiritual discipline is Awakening.

The "residue" that stays with you after a breakthrough experience such as the one described above, like most Spiritual matters, is difficult to put into words. Every time I close my eyes, I can still feel what I felt during the experience. When my eyes are closed, there is only Oneness. I can still feel what it was like to realize that I was at One with everything...literally. I still have thoughts when I'm not meditating...many...but there is something underneath the thoughts that wasn't there before. I still suffer, but there is something underneath the suffering that wasn't there before. There is an underlying sense that no matter what happens, I will be fine. Christopher Sartain may die and go away, but the real essence of what I am will remain. I **know** this. I do not believe it.

This knowledge resonates in my very Being and is not something that will ever go away. It will carry into my next life, and in my next life I will be born with this knowledge and may not have to wait thirty two years to uncover it as I did in this incarnation. We do not take meaningless transitory memories with us of trivial events from one incarnation to the next, but there are imprints, impressions, and residues left on our astral self that we do bring with us into each lifetime. This is what some traditions refer to as karma. Karma is simply what we take with us...our baggage so to speak.

Karma is what presents us with all our unique personal challenges and obstacles from one lifetime to the next. Often times it is based upon one's experiences in previous lives. However, it would seem as though we create most of our problems based upon the choices that we make in our current lifetime. In fact, I once heard a Master say in a lecture that I was attending that 90% of our present karma is due to our choices in this lifetime, and only 10% is from previous incarnations. So most of the problems that we face in our current incarnation are to be avoided and/or solved as quickly as possible so that we may focus our attention on the deeper 10% that we carry with us from previous lives. The best way to "burn off karma" is to meditate in the deep stillness and silence and merge our awareness with the Witness.

Karma from previous lives is easy to observe in the case of identical twins. Twins come from the same exact DNA and should therefore display the same exact personality characteristics, IQ, likes and dislikes, etc... This is not the case. Anyone who has ever been around identical twins can easily see that they often times display extreme differences in personality, intelligence, creativity, and temperament. This is due to the fact that each twin brings with them subconscious tendencies (karma) from previous lives into their current incarnations, which color their current personalities. In recent years, some doctors that study twins have begun to accept the reincarnation hypothesis as the only logical explanation for the differences seen in identical twins.

As I stated previously, the Witness has no physicality. Therefore, there is nothing for karma to cling to when we speak of the Witness or Pure Consciousness. When we are immersed in deep meditative states karma has nowhere to reside. Karma has some physicality, as it must adhere itself to the astral body, which is still physical even though it vibrates at a much lighter frequency than our material body. When we are at one with Witness Consciousness, there is nowhere for our karma to hang out. Karma does not exist at that level. The more time we spend diving and bathing in the ocean of Infinity, the less effect karma has on our life.

Karmic seeds, or samskaras, must take root in the field of ego. They are nourished by the ego and fed by suffering. Samskaras have a subtle physicality and must cling to something physical. Everything outside of Pure Consciousness or the Witness has physicality no matter how subtle. The only "place" where we can be free of the effects of karma is in Witness Consciousness because the Witness is immaterial and therefore samskaras literally have nowhere to take root and grow.

When we react to any situation emotionally we are feeding our samskaras. If we get angry, it is because we have a karmic seed of anger within us. If we become afraid, it is because we have a karmic seed of fear within us. If we get depressed, it is because we have a karmic seed of sadness within us. Any time we react, we water our seeds. If someone insults me, and I react, then I am watering the samskaras of anger already within me. If I instead witness my reaction, then the reaction will subside quickly. If we participate in the reaction, the reaction and emotional state lasts longer. We may never reach a point where there is no reaction at all, but we can certainly reach a state where a reaction is so short that it's barely noticeable.

The idea is to practice observing our reactions so much that it becomes second nature and eventually our true nature. We can learn to witness our emotions, thoughts, memories, and desires with complete objectivity. The trick is our sense of self-identity. Do we identify with our temporary personality self or do we identify with our Infinite Self? Do we identify with the sufferer or that which silently witnesses the sufferer? As long as we believe that we are our bodies and personalities, then we will continue to live in Spiritual ignorance and our suffering will see no end. When the identification is merged with the Infinite, suffering is impossible because the karmic seeds that are the cause of suffering have nowhere to take root or grow.

Another way of thinking about this is to consider the fact that suffering must take place in time and space. Pure Consciousness is outside the realms of time and space and yet it is the substratum for all of time and space. Without this substratum time and space could not exist. When someone is afraid, they are experiencing fear in 4D space-time. Their soul is incapable of experiencing fear because it does not exist in 4D space-time. Time is a prerequisite for suffering. We suffer due to our concept of self as it relates to time. For example, we view ourselves in terms of our past and our future. We often times suffer because of things that have occurred in the past that affected our story in a negative way. We also suffer due to worries about our future situation. Neither the past nor the future exists in ultimate Reality. That's why it is so vital to stay in the present.

Another way to practice being the Witness is to stay in the present. Staying in the present and being the Witness are the same thing. Depending on which enlightenment tradition one practices, they may hear teachers tell them to "be the Witness" and others may tell them to "stay in the present," but they are saying the same exact thing. Some seekers prefer to think of themselves as the Witness, while others prefer to think of themselves as being present. Either way is fine. They both work and have slightly different connotations so I like to teach both to my Yoga and meditation students.

Being present means that we are not focusing on our past or future, which causes suffering. Being the Witness means that we observe all phenomena with dispassionate objectivity. To not focus on past or future implies that we are witnessing, and to observe things dispassionately implies that we would give no value to past or future so they go hand in hand. However, one may be more helpful at times than the other. For instance, if I were struggling with something from my past, reminding myself to stay present would be more beneficial. If I were trying to overcome a harmful desire or addiction then witnessing the sensations in my body and mind as they arose might be more beneficial. Both being present and being the Witness, while they are the same thing, have slightly different applications on our Spiritual path. For whatever reason, I do feel as though being the Witness has a broader application than being present and that is why I have chosen to emphasize the Witness here.

Either way, being present and being the Witness both take practice. The vast majority of people living in this current Earth age do not have the innate ability to be present and/or to Witness the contents of the mind without reaction. Most of us require diligent practice. At first, not reacting to negative situations is quite difficult to master, and then not reacting to positive situations can prove even more difficult. It only feels natural to get angry when someone insults us, or to become happy when someone praises us. It feels quite unnatural the first few times we observe our anger without reaction, and even more unnatural to observe our joy without reaction. Just as it feels unnatural to be worried about the future and finances and then suddenly find yourself calmly in the present. Over time, however, it begins to feel very natural to observe our finite self without reaction. Also, the more we practice meditation, the easier it becomes to remain rooted in the present because our minds become trained not to hang out in the past or future. Spirituality is a practice…a lifelong practice. We never stop learning. As soon as we think we're done, the universe will present us with new learning opportunities for growth and evolution. There is always another rung on the ladder. We can never truly reach "perfection".

Perfection may not exist. In fact, God may not even be perfect. If God were perfect, then imperfections in his creation would be impossible and as we all know, humans are far from perfect. Therefore, if God were perfect, nothing would exist. It is imbalance, chaos, and disharmony that causes creation. It is the universe's ebb and flow and search for harmony and order out of chaos that allows all to exist and evolve. If the universe were already perfect and in harmony, none of us would exist. We are all God trying to perfect Itself and work out all the disharmonies and imbalances in the universe. We are all units of One Supreme Reality evolving towards a singularity or perfection. Evolution is impossible without imperfection and imbalance. Imperfection is a prerequisite for evolution. Since everything in the universe is constantly evolving, we can say with some certainty that the universe is imperfect and part of our role is to help God perfect Itself through our Conscious evolution on Earth. The best way to act out our role is to meditate to a state of superconsciousness daily, and then to take that state back out into the world to assist in the healing and enlightenment of all sentient beings.

Taking the Witness out in to the world is of particular importance in the age that we find ourselves. As I stated previously, there are not enough qualified Spiritual teachers in the world right now to accommodate the amount of truth seekers. That is why it is so important for meditators to go out in to the world and actively participate in it. I know many excellent meditators who are borderline hermits. I am not ok with the philosophy that says it is enough just to meditate because that cleanses the collective consciousness. While this is true, it does not help the average truth seeker on their quest in a practical sense. Most seekers require someone that they can ask questions of and see in person. Likewise, I do not believe that it is beneficial for seekers to have a deceased Guru. It is far superior to have a Guru or teacher that is alive and well that you can spend time with and ask questions of. Caves and monasteries have their place in Spirituality, but escapism and seclusion are slowly becoming less and less practical for truth seekers who would like to meditate, but who also want to maintain a full and rich Earth existence in their bodies.

Separating the Spiritually awake people from everyone else does not benefit humanity as a whole, only those practicing in caves and monasteries. Many so called "Spiritual people" live in near seclusion their entire lives and never interact with the outside world. If they do develop any enlightenment in seclusion, it is a fragile, frail enlightenment. Enlightenment that has never been tried and tested in the real world is nearly worthless. I have known of many people that go to a ten day Vipassana meditation retreat and upon their return do not want to be around any people and want to remain in seclusion and silence. That is why practices such as these resemble more the practices of a renunciate and should not be practiced too often by householders and normal lay people that have to function in society.

A daily 30-45 minute meditation practice is far superior to a ten day retreat that teaches us that peace comes when we are away from the world and silent at ten day retreats. The problem with such practices is that people become dependent upon them for peace. I know people that only have two weeks of vacation time every year and they spend almost all of it at a Vipassana retreat, instead of traveling, learning a new hobby, or spending time with friends and family. This type of Spiritual practice is self-defeating and counterproductive. If one has made the choice to be a renunciate, then long-term silent meditation retreats are fantastic, but for the vast majority of people renunciate practices have the potential to be quite harmful and damaging to one's way of life.

A much more practical and logical practice is to meditate everyday to a state of superconsciousness; then the idea of doing a ten day retreat to go meditate seems supercilious. I am not saying that an occasional retreat is not beneficial, even for householders, but so many people become dependent on retreats for their practice. For instance, I know of people that can only meditate when they are on retreat and cannot meditate at home by themselves. I know people who only meditate for ten days a year when they are at a Vipassana retreat. If meditation is a **practice**, then **practicing** three hundred and sixty five days a year is obviously much better than practicing ten days a year.

When people return from a meditation retreat and have difficulty functioning in the world and interacting with others, then I am not sure how the retreat benefitted them. If a person is a renunciate and is returning to a cave or ashram following a retreat and does not have to interact much with society then it is of no real importance, but for a householder returning back to a worldly life, it can be overwhelming. Again, there are so few teachers available right now that the world thinks it is a good idea for householders to do renunciate practices. We have lost so much common sense Spiritual knowledge due to the cross-pollination of so many traditions in the West. The good news is the Witness is neither a renunciate nor a householder! This one fact alone can eliminate a good deal of confusion in our Spiritual lives. In reality, it is neither possible to run to God, nor run away from the world. We are always God and It is not something separate that we can run to, and we may try to leave the world behind, but we will inevitably take it and our attachments to it with us wherever we may go.

There is nothing wrong with someone who chooses a life of renunciation or celibacy. However, there is something wrong with renunciates who choose a life of solitude as a means of enlightenment. Any enlightenment based on escapism that has not been tested in real world situations is fragile. I have seen people who go into seclusion for months at a time only to come back to their life completely dysfunctional. Often times, they are less equipped to deal with life than they were before their retreat or seclusion. I have also seen people really benefit from periods of seclusion that are able to reclaim their life with a new zest and enthusiasm when they return. If one does feel the need to go in to seclusion, then it should be for the benefit of others when the person comes out of seclusion. If a seeker goes into seclusion, has an experience, but never shares it with the world then what good was it?

I have spoken with many people who have benefitted greatly from prolonged meditation retreats and even tell me they enjoy the weirdness of coming back out into the world afterwards. Some people are prepared and equipped for such an experience and are quite capable of re-integrating themselves back into their normal lives, but there are others who are not quite as capable, and they require a qualified guide to help them discern the differences between renunciate and householder practices.

3 THE FIVE KOSHAS

The Five Koshas are sheaths or coverings that shadow our inner Light or Atman. The Five Koshas consist of the physical sheath (Annamaya Kosha), the energetic sheath (Pranamaya Kosha), the mental sheath (Manamaya Kosha), the ego/wisdom sheath (Vijnanamaya Kosha), and the bliss sheath (Anandamaya Kosha). Yoga philosophy when taught using the Five Koshas as the foundation is very simple and concise. Yoga in this sense is simply the process of moving through the different layers of our Being balancing and relaxing one at a time until we reach our Soul (Atman) or Pure Consciousness.

The Kosha system comes to us from the Taittirya Upanishad predating the Yoga Sutras by about one thousand years. This system for understanding the various layers of our Being is the most ancient system of its kind. The wisdom handed down to us from the Upanishads and Vedas is without equal in the ancient Spiritual and Religious lexicon. Unfortunately, the Koshas have been overlooked by modern Yoga teachers. Instead, modern practitioners prefer to focus on the Chakra system, which makes up but one of the Five Koshas. The Seven Chakras make up the second Kosha, Pranamaya Kosha. I believe that approaching Yoga philosophy from a foundation based upon the Koshas is essential for a complete understanding of Yoga as a system of Spiritual development. A holistic Yoga practice ought to encompass all five layers of our Being so that every facet of our lives improve; physically, mentally, and Spiritually.

Asana or the physical practice of Yoga works primarily on only one layer of our Being. Likewise, Pranayama, or the energetic practice of Yoga, works primarily on one layer of our Being. Mantra mediation practice also works primarily on one layer of our Being. Any holistic Yoga practice must aim to work on every layer, every Kosha. It's not enough to work on one layer at the expense of all the others. As yogis, we must endeavor to balance and master every level of our existence. Yoga is all encompassing. The goal of Yoga is the bringing together of all layers of our Being into Divine Union with Infinite Consciousness.

In many systems of Yoga and Spiritual practice, one layer of our Being is the primary focus at the exclusion of the others. For instance, I know of Spiritual traditions that are not at all "body friendly". Their only concern is the Infinite soul at the expense of all else. Some of these traditions even practice forms of self punishment and bodily mutilation as a way to repent for their sins or bad karma. There are some ascetic traditions that allow only a few morsels of rice a day for weeks at a time while undergoing severe fasts. We must take care of every layer of our Being, even the physical body. For it is the vessel of the soul, and without it enlightenment is impossible. How can we expect to arrive at our destination if our car is in disrepair?

The first Kosha is Annamaya Kosha, or the physical body. Anna means food. Maya means illusion. All of the Koshas end in the word Maya, because all of physical reality is just an illusion after all. The only "thing" that is real is Pure Consciousness due to its unchanging nature. The physical sheath consists primarily of our most dense layer, the body with all its matter. Everyone is familiar with this layer and it requires little explanation.

The next of the koshas is Pranamaya Kosha. Prana means energy. This Kosha is generally associated with the subtle body or energy body. This is where we experience, send, and receive emotions and energies. For instance, when you walk into a room with bad energy or a bad vibe and you immediately feel it, that is your energy body experiencing the bad vibe. Likewise, when you sit in front of a Guru and your Heart Chakra nearly explodes, it is your energetic body feeling the Guru's Shaktipat, or Divine energy.

The next of the Koshas is Manamaya Kosha. Manas means mind. It is the level of processing thoughts and emotions. This is where our thinking, fantasizing, remembering, and decision making occurs. The Soul needs the mind in order to experience Itself. It is a tool that can be used to make choices, which lead one closer to the Divine.

The next of the Koshas is Vijnanamaya Kosha. Vijnana means knowing. It is the sheath of wisdom or ego that is underneath the processing, thinking aspect of mind. It is the level of ego consciousness, meaning the powerful wave of I-am-ness. This I-am-ness itself is a positive influence, but when it gets co-mingled with memories, and is clouded over by the Manas, it loses its positive power.

Anandamaya Kosha is the most interior of the Koshas, the first of the Koshas surrounding the Atman, the eternal center of Consciousness. Ananda means bliss. However, it is not bliss as a mere emotion experienced at the level of the sheath of mind. Ananda is a whole different order of reality from that of the mind. It is peace, joy, and love that exists underneath the layer of mind, independent of any reason or stimulus to cause a happy mental reaction.

Atman is the Self, the eternal center of Consciousness, which was never born and never dies. In a metaphor using a lamp and lampshades, Atman is the Light itself. The deepest Light shines through the Koshas (lampshades), and takes on their colorings. This is what gives each one of us our unique individuality.

Yoga may be defined as the process of moving through each Kosha, balancing and relaxing one at a time until the practitioner reaches the core of their Being. Patanjali in his Yoga Sutras gives us an exact formula for transcending each Kosha one at a time until we attain Samadhi and reach the Witness, Infinite Consciousness, God, or whatever we choose to call it.

In the second section of the Yoga Sutras, Patanjali lays out for us the Eight Limbs of Yoga. The first two limbs deal with the Yamas and Niyamas, which essentially amount to a ten commandments-like list of moral laws to be followed by Yoga practitioners. The difference between Patanjali and the Old-testament is that Patanjali does not stop there. After he gives us a moral code to follow, he then proceeds to give us a formula for developing and improving our morality and enlightenment. So it is basically just like the ten commandments, but in addition we get a step by step instruction manual to go along with them.

It's one thing to tell someone not to steal, murder, covet, etc...but it's another thing all together to alter someone's personality and Being in such a way that they would never want to steal, murder, or covet again. The goal of Yoga is not to give us a strict moral code and then leave us on our own. Instead, Yoga offers a clear scientific approach to becoming a better person, one Kosha at a time.

Limbs 3-8 deal with the steps in the process of Yoga. Each step is meant to help us balance and transcend each Kosha one at a time. The steps are as follows: 1)Asana, 2)Pranayama, 3)Pratyahara, 4)Dharana, 5)Dhyana, 6)Samadhi. Asana means physical postures, Pranayama means breathing techniques, Pratyahara means control of the senses, Dharana means concentration, Dhyana means meditation, and Samadhi is Oneness with ultimate Reality. By using the formula put forth by Patanjali two thousand years ago, one may work through each layer of their Being until they reach Samadhi, or Oneness Consciousness. So much Yoga in the West focuses on Asana (physical postures) alone to the exclusion of all the other steps in the process. This has left the Western world with a confused view of Yoga as a Spiritual practice. This is because many supposed Yoga practitioners are only doing one limb out of the eight when they practice. For any real Spiritual benefit, it is essential to practice all eight limbs.

We use Asana to balance and transcend the physical layer, Pranayama to balance and transcend the energetic layer, Pratyahara and Dharana to balance and transcend the mental layer, Dhyana to balance and transcend the ego layer, and Samadhi to transcend the bliss layer ultimately reaching our Infinite core. This is the basic premise and process of Yoga as described by Patanjali in the Yoga

Sutras and it is a process that has as much applicability today as it did in his time in ancient India. Yoga provides us with a scientific approach to life and Spirituality that has no equal. Many systems have come and gone, but for some reason, the Sacred Science of Yoga and Meditation have managed to stand the test of time lasting for well over five thousand years. If something sticks around for five thousand years, it's because it works.

4 ANNAMAYA KOSHA & ASANA

In the West, Yoga is typically thought of as a physical practice. However, historically, Yoga has been anything but. In fact, in Patanjali's Yoga Sutras there is only one mention of Asana. In sutra 2.46 Patanjali states that "the meditation posture should be comfortable and stable." And in the following sutra we are told that the posture "becomes stable as concentration flows effortlessly and awareness blends with God-consciousness." And in the Bhagavad Gita there is also brief mention of proper meditation posture, but all it really says is to "hold the body, head, and neck erect." Therefore, it can be ascertained from the ancient texts that asana in ancient times was associated primarily with a seated meditation posture. It was not until the 11th century with the writings of Gorakhnath that we find mention of asanas not having to do with seated mediation postures. In the 15th century the Hatha Yoga Pradipika gives a little more instruction in physical asana practice, but it still bears no resemblance whatsoever to our modern day asana practice found in gyms and studios the world over.

Our modern asana practice can trace its roots back to a man from south India named Krishnamacharya. He developed a system of vinyasa flow Yoga that forms the basis of our current physical asana practice. Vinyasa is a type of Yoga that flows with the breath. Prior to this, it was common to simply hold one asana for an extended period, and then move to another one and so on, but vinyasa combines movement with the breath. Sun salutations are probably the most obvious example of vinyasa flow. Krishnamacharya was heavily influenced by the European gymnastics becoming popular in early 20th century India, and in particular Dutch gymnastics and stretching. We derive many of our modern asanas from these gymnastics routines.

Krishnamacharya is attributed with creating and founding Ashtanga Yoga and was the teacher of B.K.S. Iyengar and Sri K. Pattabhi Jois who went on to be the two most widely regarded and important Yoga teachers of their generation. The teachings of these men have spawned a menagerie of spin-offs and self styled traditions, such as Bikram Yoga and the like. There are more Yoga styles and traditions now than anyone can keep track of. What we now think of as asana is a very recent phenomenon. It has only existed as such for less than a century. Anyone who tells you otherwise has not done their homework. This is not an ancient practice as many have stated. However, I do not mean to take away from the beneficial nature of the modern practice or diminish its importance simply because it isn't ancient.

Our modern Yoga practice is a true blessing and has many health benefits. I certainly do not mean to imply that every class happening in gyms and studios is high quality and "good for you", but that the practice itself as handed down from Krishnamacharya and his successors was something that was missing from a well rounded Yoga practice. Why shouldn't we have a physical practice to calm and balance the physical layer of our Beings as preparation for deeper work? I love practicing a physically engaging asana sequence prior to pranayama and meditation. I find that my meditations are always much, much deeper after a 30-45 minute asana practice. This follows along with the premise that we ought to move through each layer of our Being one at a time relaxing and balancing each, until we arrive at our true nature. Perhaps in ancient times practitioners' bodies and nervous systems were more relaxed and balanced and that is why they did not practice asana as we do today. Or perhaps they did have a more vigorous physical practice that has been lost with the sands of time.

Either way, asana has come to be a vital part of our modern Yoga practice and it should be treated with the same amount of respect as the higher practices of pranayama or meditation. In fact it should be treated as necessary preparation for pranayama and meditation. So much of our meditation experience depends upon the state or condition of the spine and nervous system. The relaxation and balancing of the spine that comes about as a result of all the twisting and stretching via asana allows for prana and high vibrational energies to travel along the spine without obstruction. That is why I highly recommend chiropractic adjustments regularly for serious yogis.

My entire practice and Consciousness shifted considerably after my first chiropractic adjustment. I had already been practicing Yoga for several years and I had developed some pain in my left shoulder and hip. That's when someone told me about chiropractic spinal adjustments. I went to my local chiropractor and he adjusted every bone in my body it seemed; it was a bit scary the first time I went, especially the first time I had my neck done! Following the adjustment, I had a complete energetic shift. Creative energies that had been locked dormant were unleashed, and I also found that I needed to meditate less after the adjustment. I also suddenly found myself wanting to be more social and outgoing. So much of our energetic/emotional condition is tied to the condition of the spine and nervous system. Had I known this earlier, I would have sought out a chiropractor much sooner in life, but everything happens when it's ready to happen.

I also highly recommend massage in addition to chiropractic and Yoga asana. I am sure the reader is beginning to think that this is going to be expensive, but consider what many people spend on their vices every month when they could be transmuting that money into massages, Yoga asana classes, and chiropractic adjustments. Just one massage a month, one adjustment a month, and one Yoga class a week is plenty to get started. Although, I would suggest doing a little asana at home every day, especially first thing in the morning just prior to pranayama and meditation. But one group class a week is a good idea to stay motivated. The group dynamic of regularly attending classes helps us stay focused and inspired to practice at home. The same can be said for a weekly group meditation gathering.

The best way to cultivate a healthy annamaya kosha is to adhere to an Ayurvedic lifestyle and vegetarian-organic diet. Ayurveda could be considered the ninth limb of Yoga. It is the most ancient healing system on Earth and goes hand in hand with Yoga practice. Understanding one's Dosha, or mind-body constitution can have a significant and lasting impact on the overall health of one's body. There are three Doshas, which can be thought of as mind-body constitutions, of which we are all constructed. However, each of us express one Dosha more dominantly over the other two, generally speaking. This is said to be our dominant Dosha or type. The three Doshas are Vata, Pitta, and Kapha. Our dominant Dosha plays a role in all aspects of our physical life from what types of foods we should be eating to what types of Yoga we should be doing. For instance, someone who is a pitta-type should probably stay away from "hot-yoga", as the heat can exacerbate pitta conditions and tendencies.

Vata means "wind, to move, flow, direct the processes of, or command." The actions of vata are drying, cooling, light, agitating, and moving. It sustains effort, inhalation and exhalation, circulation, movements of impulses, tissue balance, and coordination of the senses. Its primary seat in the body is the colon. Vata, being a combination of ether and air influences, is present and influential where there are spaces in which Prana can move. Regular exercise should be relaxed and moderate for vata-types. Yoga should be practiced in a slow, intentional, meditative mood. Tai chi, walking, swimming and other non-frantic activities are also good for vatas.

Pitta means "fire". It heats, digests, and is influential in chemical and metabolic transformations. Being a combination of fire and water elements, it is present in the body in moistures and oils, and in the fluids of the digestive system and blood. Pitta's primary seat or location in the body is the small intestine. Pittas should practice Yoga in a room with a normal temperature, and avoid heated classes over 90 degrees. It is also best for pitta-types to avoid classes with a competitive atmosphere such as advanced Ashtanga and vinyasa classes. People who express pitta dominantly are often the ones we see in class peering over at their neighbors to compare poses. Therefore, any notion of competition either with others or oneself is to be avoided altogether for pittas, especially as it concerns their Yoga asana practice.

Kapha is a combination of water and earth elements and is present in the body as moisture and dense substances. It holds things together. Mucus, for instance, indicates its influence in the body. Kapha Dosha provides nourishment, substance, and support, and makes up the mass of the body's tissues and its lubricating aspects. Kapha Dosha effects are mostly cold, moist, heavy, and slow. Kapha-types tend to be heavy set, and when out of balance, obese. It is of utmost importance for kaphas to do a regular asana practice. Kaphas should engage in a vigorous, aerobic style of asana such as a power flow class. Hot yoga is great for kaphas and they should be encouraged to sweat as often as possible.

Our dominant Dosha or our mind-body constitution plays a large role not only in our asana practice, but also in our choice of foods and supplements. In general, there are some Ayurvedic guidelines that are good for all three Dosha-types to follow. For instance, it is good to limit oneself to only the appropriate amount of caloric intake each day and not over-eat. Over-eating taxes our system so much that it drains the body of vital prana and energy. This is why we feel so tired after huge meals. Some life extension researchers have proven that it's actually best to take in slightly fewer calories than what is typically thought of as normal. Sometimes this is referred to as a "restricted calorie diet". The idea being that if one consumes slightly less than what the body normally requires then the body will not have to work as hard to digest and process food, and over time this surplus of energy will lead to a longer and healthier life.

A vegetarian diet is recommended for people serious about their Spiritual path. Also, a diet free of processed and artificial foods is also recommended. Plants and animals, like us, possess different layers or koshas to their Beings. The higher the organism and the more complex the nervous system and brain, the more koshas the organism develops through the process of bio-spiritual evolution. Mammals therefore are Spiritually and energetically much more related to us than broccoli for instance. We know that mammals have emotions and are capable of love and compassion. Therefore, we know they possess an astral body or pranamaya kosha, even if it isn't quite as evolved as ours. It stands to reason that this astral body affects and inter-penetrates the physical body of a cow, for example, in much the same way it does in a human. The emotional state of a mammal affects the body of a mammal. When we get overstressed or frightened we release adrenaline and hormones into the bloodstream that have a nasty effect on our nervous system and body. When cows are shot in the face with a shotgun for example, they release the same nasty chemical soup into their system and it gets lodged into their tissues and cells. When people take that same flesh into their systems, it has a physical and energetic effect on their bodies that is often times so subtle that it's difficult to detect until one completely stops eating meat. The problem is, eating meat not only affects our annamaya kosha or physical body in a negative way, but it also has a negative effect on our pranamaya kosha, or energetic/astral body. One could even make the case that it affects our manamaya kosha or mental body in a negative way due to its dulling and violence-enhancing effects on the mind. With all the meat alternatives and protein powders, etc. on the market right now, especially in industrialized countries, there is no rational excuse for eating meat. Vegetarians live an average of 7-15 years longer than meat eaters in most studies that have been done, and are far less likely to develop cancer, diabetes, and other dietary related diseases.

In addition to eating light and adhering to a vegetarian or vegan diet, it is also important to eat for your type. There are many wonderful books already available on Ayurvedic diet plans tailored for the Three Doshas specifically so I won't go into any great detail here, but needless to say avoiding problem foods for one's type is highly beneficial when on a Spiritual path. For instance, if someone that is pitta-dominant knows that they tend to get angry (a typical pitta trait) when they eat hot spicy foods, then they can avoid those foods in the future. Likewise, if a kapha person tends to get lazy when they eat too much dairy, then they can avoid foods with cheese and milk while adhering to daily exercise routines to gain more energy and motivation for their Spiritual pursuits.

A balanced, varied, and well proportioned diet is necessary preparation for asana. Without a healthy diet, a healthy body is impossible and without a healthy body, asana is made far more difficult. A light, healthy vegetarian diet goes hand in hand with a solid asana practice. It would be hard, for instance, to gobble down a Big Mac and then go do a demanding hour and a half asana class right after. Being mindful about what and when we eat is a vital part of any Yoga practice. In fact, one should not eat anything two hours prior to practicing asana. That's why it is a great idea to practice some asana first thing in the morning before we have had time to eat anything when our body is lightest and cleanest.

Treat the body with respect. After all, we are all God manifesting in multi-layer physical form so we should take care of our temple and keep it clean. It is best to avoid any toxic substances or foods, especially things like alcohol, tobacco, and other drugs that may dull the system. Even certain drugs that may seem to have rather enlightening effects at first, over time will begin to dull and damage the nervous system and the regular use of psychedelic substances is not advisable for serious yogis. Even things as simple as over the counter medicines, coffee, chocolate, garlic, onions, spicy foods, etc. can really aggravate parts of our energetic and physical systems. Yogis must be mindful of what they put into their bodies at all times. Through genuine Samadhi experience, one is given the great insight that the physical and Spiritual are One. Therefore, the body is God too. When we think of the body as such, it becomes much easier to treat it with the respect it deserves.

In general, asana should be practiced in a clean and quiet space where one can remain undisturbed for the duration of practice. A nice yoga mat is a great luxury to have and it is something that every yogi should invest a little money in. Mats made with organic rubber and fair trade practices are best. When not being used, a practitioner's mat ought to be kept clean and rolled up neatly. Practicing yoga on carpet is not advisable. Hard wood floors or solid surfaces are best for placing a Yoga mat upon. The practitioner should practice bare foot at all times with loose comfortable clothing that is easy to move around in, but that doesn't "bunch up" easily either. The best colors to practice Yoga in are white and/or orange. White represents the purity of Infinite Consciousness that is the ultimate aim of our practice, and orange represents the agni, tapas, or fire that burns off our karma during practice, just as the summer sun burns off the haze of the morning cloud cover.

I once read in a book entitled <u>Long Pilgrimage</u> by John G. Bennett about the life and teachings of the Shivapuri Baba that the great Master loved to burn incense at all times. As soon as one stick would go out, he would immediately light another all day, every day. This was part of his practice because he said that it constantly purified the space and made it more Divine. The Shivapuri Baba lived to be one hundred and thirty seven years old so I think he may have been on to something. Incense, especially sandalwood, can be burned as often as one likes during their practice if it is tolerated. Environment is important. Space is important. I have found that "smudging" the space before I practice also has an uplifting, sattvic effect. One may use sage or sweet grass to bless a space prior to starting a Yoga practice or ceremony or ritual of any kind. However, some people have a sensitivity to any particles in the air, and one should use moderation when burning anything indoors that might be inhaled. People with lung and respiratory conditions such as asthma and COPD should not burn anything indoors.

Having a specific space set aside for our Spiritual practice is crucial to our success on the path. It is important to have a special place in our home that is used only for Yoga and meditation and nothing else, even if it is just a corner of a room and not an entire room. Many Masters have stated that one need not rush to the mountains to find a meditation cave. One can just as easily have a "meditation cave" in their own home. It is also nice, but not necessary, to have photos of saints and Masters on your altar space. Doing these things will imbue the area with a sattvic, or uplifting, vibration conducive to higher states of Consciousness. The more time one spends meditating in a specific spot, the higher the vibration in that spot will become. If we are fortunate enough to have the opportunity to spend time in a space where a Master has meditated often, we should take full advantage. The Shakti, or Divine healing energy, in such places is tangible and has an energetically uplifting quality.

A daily Yoga asana practice may last anywhere from thirty minutes to two hours. One should practice in a meditative mood undistracted. Soothing music may be played during the asana session if one wishes, but it should be completely silent for pranayama and meditation. There is a science to the sequencing of an asana session. One should begin with either a seated or standing warm-up before moving into sun salutations and standing flow (including warrior poses, triangle poses, etc.). After the standing series, one should move into balance postures and from there to the floor for core work, backbends, forward folds, inversions, twists, and finally savasana, in that order. This general sequence has an energetic flow and science to it that seems to work well. One can modify this sequence and tweak it a little to their liking, but this basic flow is effective preparation for pranayama and meditation. It engages and relaxes every part of the body, especially the spine and nervous system, so that pranayama and meditation flow more easily.

I like to start my asana practice with a short seated warm up including neck and shoulder stretches, side stretches, seated twists and usually a round or two of "breath of fire" pranayama. This pranayama should be taught to a practitioner by a professional yogi or yogini and should not be learned in a book. I then like to come into hand and knees, or "table top", as some like to call it. Here, I enjoy doing a few hip rolls, hand and knees bow, and "cat/cow". From hands and knees I typically drop into down dog for a few breaths and then walk my feet up to a standing forward fold. After coming up to mountain pose, or standing, I flow into five to ten rounds of sun salutations including various standing postures like warriors and triangles into the flow. Balancing postures follow the standing series; I generally prefer to do tree or dancer. I then find my way to the floor for some core work; typically forearm planks and side forearm planks. It makes sense to prepare and engage the core just prior to flowing into the backbends that follow. For backbends I like sphinx or bridge. To complement or counter the backbends, I flow into seated forward folds as a "counter pose". Backbends and core work heat up the system and spine and forward folds cool it down and prepare it for relaxation and savasana. After forward folds is a nice time to do inversions like shoulder stand or headstand. But I honestly never personally do or teach headstand, and I prefer to just do "legs at the wall" for about five minutes instead, followed by a brief half-shoulder stand or plow. After inversions, it is appropriate to balance the hemispheres of the body as preparation for final relaxation or savasana. To balance the hemispheres, supine twists, or twists lying on your back, can be done just before savasana. I like to stay in savasana for only about five minutes prior to pranayama or meditation. If I lay there too long, I am prone to getting sleepy, as are most people. So it is important in our private practice not to lie in savasana for too long if we plan to meditate afterward. Otherwise, one can stay in savasana for as long as they like.

After a short savasana, the practitioner should sit up very slowly and come to a seated, crossed legged position. If one cannot sit in half lotus, or even cross legged then just sitting upright in any comfortable position after savasana is fine. Once seated, it is time for pranayama. If there is music playing, it should be stopped and any incense should be extinguished and should not inhibit pranayama in any way. Seated upright with the spine erect and the attention in the third eye, the practitioner is ready for pranayama and meditation practice and the asana session has reached its completion, although the meditation posture or asana is of equal importance and one should remain mindful of their posture during pranayama and meditation as part of their asana practice.

The basic asana sequence that I have laid out here can be modified for any type or level of practitioner to meet their specific needs. Any decent Yoga instructor certified by the Yoga Alliance or another reputable body who has been teaching for at least two years should be capable of guiding anyone through a basic flow as I have described above. This basic sequence should be the basis and foundation of any complete and holistic asana practice. If one part of it is left out, like the forward folds for instance, then energetically and physically the sequence will feel incomplete. One must follow every step of the sequence, or there is a chance that pranayama and meditation will not go quite a well as they could have otherwise.

There is a reason for each step of a proper asana sequence, and it is all physical and energetic preparation for the rest of the practice. We will see in the next chapter that pranayama has much to do with the spine and nervous system, so without properly preparing the spine and nervous system through asana we are not providing ourselves with the highest opportunity for success with pranayama and ultimately with meditation. All of the lengthening, core work, stretching, and twisting that we do in our asana sequence strengthens the spine and nervous system and gets it ready for the higher levels of practice that follow.

Depending on how much time one has in their personal life to devote to their practice, one should devote at least thirty minutes a day to a complete asana sequence. Forty five minutes is preferable if it is available, but an hour or more is not necessary unless one is really devoted to their physical practice. Forty five minutes is a sufficient amount of time to complete a holistic asana sequence as preparation for approximately five to ten minutes of pranayama, and fifteen to forty five minutes of meditation, again depending on how much time one has in their life to devote to such practices. With our modern day hectic schedules, it is impossible for many of us to devote an hour a day to anything, let alone our Spiritual practice. I have found, however, that if one is truly serious about their path, it is possible to make time each morning and/or evening for Spiritual practice. When students tell me that they just cannot find the time for their practice, I often ask them how much time they spend watching television on a day to day basis. Many of them tell me that they regularly watch up to two hours a day of television. Obviously, this time would be better spent in the meditation cave burning off samskaras, rather than sitting in front of the great samskara seeder.

Asana calms, relaxes, and balances the annamaya kosha or physical layer of our Being. Since the annamaya kosha is the densest of layers, it requires quite a bit of physical action to calm and relax it. Whereas pranayama requires much less physical effort, mantra even less, and finally meditation with as little physical effort as possible. We work our way through each layer using less and less physical effort as we move into lighter and lighter layers that have less and less physicality to them. The koshas may be thought of as existing on something akin to the electromagnetic spectrum. As we move our way through the koshas towards Infinite Consciousness, the frequency of each kosha becomes lighter and lighter until there is no frequency, no vibration at all. All that is left in the end is what my Teacher, Roy Eugene Davis, likes to call "Pure Existence Being."

5 PRANAMAYA KOSHA AND PRANAYAMA

The pranamaya kosha is known by many names; astral body, subtle body, etheric body, energetic body, rainbow body, and vital body. The pranamaya kosha can be thought of as an energetic double of our physical body. It is like an etheric light-emitting cloud hovering around our body that can increase and decrease in size and vitality based upon our emotional state and mood. We can also expand the size of the pranamaya kosha through Yogic practices such as asana, pranayama, meditation, and chanting. Because the energetic body is just a frequency down from the physical body, it has more "physicality" to it than the remainder of the koshas. This is why we can often times see or sense the energetic body in the form of a person's aura.

The exact anatomy of the pranamaya kohsa is ambiguous and difficult to understand on a cognitive level. Many metaphysicists and Masters have left us with only morsels and crumbs with which we must reconstruct an entire meal. However, there are a few things that most traditions will agree on. There seem to exist several energy "centers" in the astral body that correspond with different energetic frequencies and sacred geometric vibratory patterns. In the Yoga tradition, these energy centers are referred to as the Seven Chakras. Other systems include more chakras, but needless to say, it is fairly well agreed upon at this point in time that humans possess an energetic or astral body of some type comprised of various transmitter/receiver centers that emit a range of vibratory frequencies now detectable by certain scientific equipment that is able to measure subtle energies.

Each chakra is related to specific emotions and parts of our psyche. Our base chakra located around the base of the spine is associated with survival instincts and fear. When in balance our base chakra leaves us with a sense of security; when out of balance, a sense of insecurity. The second chakra is associated with our sexual and creative energy. When in balance we experience a normal sex life; when out of balance, we either over indulge in sexual activity or avoid sex altogether. The third chakra is associated will power and is located opposite the navel. When in balance the third chakra gives us the strength that we need to move through the world. When out of balance, we either give in to too many worldly pleasures, or we avoid life, duty, and responsibility, and/or we attempt to exert our power over others. The fourth chakra is the heart chakra. This is the most noticeable and obvious of the chakras as we have all felt the pain of heartache over the loss of someone or something valuable in our lives and we've all felt the warmth in our hearts when we are around loved ones. When in balance we are able to give and receive love equally and abundantly. When out of balance, we are not good receivers, or we are not good givers. The fifth chakra is the throat chakra and is associated with truth. When in balance this chakra expresses as honesty; when out of balance, dishonesty. The sixth chakra is the third eye. This is where we can experience higher states of reality and send and receive telepathic messages. It is where Yoga meditators hold their attention during meditation practice. When in balance we are given powers of a psychic nature; when out of balance, we only see and experience a limited reality in the 4D plane. The seventh chakra is the crown chakra. This is where we experience superconsciousness and Samadhi, the highest states of Yogic practice. When in balance this chakra gives us enlightened states of consciousness; when out of balance, Spiritual ignorance.

Our chakras can be thought of as the strings on an instrument like a guitar. Each string vibrates at a different frequency and each string must be tuned to the proper frequency or the guitar will not sound right. Likewise, we must tune our chakras so that they resonate appropriately with one another so that the entire instrument (the pranamaya kosha) will function properly. Pranayama is the means by which we tune our chakra system so that our energetic body functions at its highest capacity. I have given here a gross oversimplification of the chakra system, simply because it is beyond the scope of this book, but for further reading on the matter, I highly recommend <u>Eastern Body Western Mind</u> by Anodea Judith.

There are two paths to enlightenment. One is via the mind through realization, the other is via the energy body through Kundalini awakening. Sometimes these two paths meet, and other times they occur separately. One is not necessarily superior to the other and both lead to the same ultimate destination. The means of enlightenment via the energy body is possible due to our physical body. This path begins in the physical body through intense purification. Without a clean and well functioning nervous system, one can forget about the possibility of a full Kundalini awakening. It simply is not possible. Once the body has been purified through a strict natural vegetarian diet, asana, pranayama, meditation and Samadhi, then one can begin thinking about the possibility of an energetic awakening. This is why real full Kundalini awakenings are so rare in this day and age; our planet is too polluted. How can we expect to purify our physical bodies when we live in an impure environment? It is quite difficult in our current era, but I believe that is all about to change drastically as geniuses begin to unleash "free-energy devices" as alternatives to our fossil fuel dependency. This will have a major impact on the global environment, as will the re-localization of our food supplies as we move away from giant corporate agriculture (again, beyond the scope of this book).

When the environment is right, and the body is properly attended to, energetic awakenings are far easier. In our current era, it would seem as though there are more people awakening due to realizations that occur at the level of mind. Samadhi can be brought about by either means, and as I stated before, often times when Masters fully awaken it is a combination of energetic and mental. My only experience with a high state of Samadhi most definitely included various happenings within my energetic body, so it is more complicated than our minds can grasp logically. Once in Samadhi, one's awareness is brought out beyond either the mental or energetic body into Pure Infinite Consciousness; merged entirely with the Witness or Oneness so the means are just the means. It is the end result that deserves our fullest attention. The same can be said of mediation. My Teacher, Roy Eugene Davis, likes to say that mediation technique is arbitrary from the standpoint of Samadhi. It is simply a means to an end and people put far too much emphasis on technique. It is very important, but not worth bickering over with people from other traditions. We should simply find what techniques work best for us and use them to the best of our ability.

During a Kundalini awakening there is a Divine nectar that is created in the brain that the ancient Indians referred to as Soma. It has been known by many names throughout the ages; the manna, the philosopher's stone, the sacred oil, etc... Even the word Christos or Christ means "anointed". One who has been anointed with the sacred oil has achieved the state of "Christos".

My brain secretes this Soma nearly every time I sit to meditate and it has been a little difficult to get used to, especially when it first started happening because I had no idea what it was. That's why it is so helpful to have a qualified teacher. All I had to do was send Roy an email and he told me why it was occurring, and that it was just a natural part of meditating. I can feel it dripping down from my brain into my mouth and creating a very pleasant tasting saliva. It is important to swallow this nectar, as it has a rejuvanative, cleansing effect on the body. During an energetic awakening this Soma drips down the spine to the very base where it awakens the sleeping Kundalini serpent and wrests the great dragon guarding its gold from the cave. I would define Kundalini as the evolutionary force of Consciousness. It is what propels us forward and brings us into closer union with the Divine.

Once this Divine Soma seeds and awakens the coiled and dormant Kundalini energy, there is an alchemical reaction that occurs in the energetic body. The serpent energy is brought up the sushumna nadi or central highway in our astral system. As it moves up the sushumna nadi, it tunes, clears, purifies, and energizes each chakra on its way up. When this is occurring, it is common for people to have intense visions of a vivid or psychedelic nature; each vision being associated with each individual chakra and all that it represents. Once the Kundalini climaxes at the crown chakra, there is an explosion of Divine energy and one experiences the highest state of ecstasy and bliss imaginable. However, if one becomes "stuck" here due to the feeling of bliss, they will not experience Oneness Consciousness. One must even transcend the bliss of God-communion to experience the ultimate Oneness of all.

One time Roy asked Yogananda how many of the saints and sages that he had known throughout his lifetime were fully liberated. Yogananda replied, "Oh, not many." He went on say that most were content to revel in the bliss of God-communion and so they never "went all the way." But then Yogananda told Roy that he must "go all the way in this lifetime and you can do it!" It is important not to take for granted our current incarnation. It is a gift and its potential should be maximized. One would not be wise to adhere to the philosophy that we have many incarnations to awaken and so there is no rush. The sooner one awakens, the less they have to suffer and live in ignorance.

The astral planes look very different from our normal reality. Yogananda describes the astral planes in the following passage:

The astral planes are of differing atmospheres, or vibrations, and each soul that passes on from this earth is attracted to whichever atmosphere is in harmony with its own particular vibration. Just as fish live in water, worms in the earth, man on the earth, and birds in the air, so souls in the astral world live in whichever sphere is best suited to their own vibration. The more noble and spiritual a person is on earth, the higher the sphere to which he will be attracted, and the greater will be his freedom and joy and experience of beauty.

On the astral planets, beings are not dependent upon air or electricity in order to exist. They live in variously coloured rays of light. There is more freedom in the astral world than in the physical world. There are no bones to break, because there are no solids there; everything is composed of light rays. And everything takes place by the power of thought. When souls in the astral want to produce a garden, they merely will it, and the garden comes into being. It remains as long as it is willed to. When a soul wants the garden to disappear, it goes away.

One may reincarnate to a higher astral plane as Yogananda describes through the process of Ascension. This is where we no longer have any need for a physical form for the time being and can come and go between the various planes or dimensions as we please for the most part. At some point most souls are attracted back into a physical world of form, but it is certainly possible to ascend to higher and higher planets, planes, and/or dimensions as we evolve Spiritually.

In the Kriya Yoga tradition of which I am a part, we do not emphasize beliefs about reincarnation. This is because Roy Eugene Davis prefers to emphasize Awakening in this life time in the Here and Now. He believes that focusing on reincarnation and things such as "past-life recall" are a waste of time. Instead, Roy believes that we should focus our attention on our current incarnation and not wait for future incarnations to Awaken.

My wife and I had the good fortune of having a Tibetan Lama named Tenzin Lama Sherpa come stay with us for a few weeks in October of 2012. He is a wonderful meditation master from Nepal. He lived in Chile for a short time and my wife is from Chile so when they met here in the United States they immediately had that in common and became fast friends. I was blessed enough to have private one on one conversations with him every evening in our home about a great many topics.

In our conversations there was an emphasis on the astral body and on different metaphysical energies and dimensions. In the Tibetan tradition the astral body is called the rainbow body. When a high Lama or Rinpoche dies they have an opportunity to ascend and shed the physical body and attain a rainbow body. Tenzin Lama showed me videos taken at Indian and Nepalese monasteries where there appear giant circular rainbows in the sky hovering over holy sites and temples usually following the death of a high Lama or Rinpoche. In these videos, there are no clouds in the sky. In other words, there are no natural causes for these rainbows. Tenzin Lama explained that this was a sign that a Master had ascended and attained their rainbow body.

The footage in the videos is remarkable and could be evidence that the miraculous is alive and well in our world. I have seen many miraculous events in my lifetime and so have millions of other people. Any notion that we are in some type of "dense" age or "dark" age and cannot experience the miraculous in the present is absurd. I am fine with the idea that there have been more enlightened ages on planet Earth and that there will be again in the future, but that does not mean that we are somehow incapable of experiencing the miraculous in the Here and Now. For an enlightening look into the cycles of ages called the Yugas in the Vedic tradition read The Holy Science by Sri Yukteswar, Yogananda's Guru.

To calm and balance our pranamaya kosha we use pranayama. Pranayama is the science of the breath and prana control. Prana is generally defined as life-force energy. It is what gives us life and is therefore inextricably linked to the breath. We take in prana from food, herbs, water, air, the sun, and the Earth. Unlike Kundalini energy, prana is kinetic and moving at all times. Kundalini on the other hand is potential energy lying dormant at the base of the spine awaiting arousal and impregnation. Prana is that which gives life its vitality and animation. We die because we run out of prana.

We can increase or decrease the amount of prana in the body at any given time. We increase our level of prana through proper diet and exercise, yoga asana, pranayama, meditation, and chanting. We decrease the level of prana in our bodies through stress, poor diet, lack of exercise, lack of sleep, too much sensual stimulation, anger, fear, worry, addiction, depression, etc... In fact, most people in our modern day world are walking around with severely depleted levels of prana and are not even aware of it; usually until they take their first Yoga class and feel more "vital" than they have in a long time. This is because they have literally increased the level of prana in their energetic body, which has a positive effect on the physical and mental bodies as well.

There are many wonderful pranayamas that have various different effects on the practitioner. Pranayamas, even the simplest ones, should be taught in person by a yogi advanced in pranayama practice. These techniques are quite powerful and should not be learned in a book. One may attain some degree of proficiency learning pranayama from videos, but one on one personal instruction from a qualified teacher is far superior. All pranayama techniques should be practiced in a calm, meditative state with full attention given to the breath. In giving our full attention to the breath for pranayama, we are removing the senses from externals and preparing the mind for mantra and meditation practice. Remember, there is a sequential order to a complete and holistic Yoga routine. It starts by balancing the body with asana, and then moves on to balancing the energetic body with pranayama, the mental body with mantra, the ego/wisdom body with mediation, and the bliss body with Samadhi so that we may uncover our eternal core.

Kundalini Yoga as developed by Yogi Bhajan consists of many intense pranayamas that should most assuredly be learned by a trained yogi in that tradition. I can personally attest to the power of pranayama and its effects on the energetic sheath. About three years ago, I was in bed about to fall asleep and I had just taken my first Kundalini Yoga class in Birmingham, Alabama with a student of Yogi Bhajan's. It was two hours of the most intense pranayama that I had ever done, followed by about two hours of Sanskrit chanting. As I was falling asleep, I became aware of the state in between sleep and waking. I was in that in between state and my mind felt very "loose". Suddenly, something prompted me to gaze intently into my third eye. I looked as hard as I could into my third eye for a few seconds and then out of nowhere it was like I saw into Infinity and then Infinity collapsed in on Itself and rushed back into my third eye all at once. As soon as Infinity had folded back in on Itself and thrust Itself into my forehead, my spine shot straight up. I have never felt my spine move on its own volition and straighten and crack like that. It was a little scary at the time to be honest.

My neck then cracked and straightened and before I knew it I was sitting straight up in bed half asleep not of my own accord. Something besides my conscious self was making this happen. After my spine straightened and I was sitting upright, a surge of energy rushed up my sushumna nadi and out my crown chakra. It was like an energetic explosion had just occurred in my astral body. And then something I never expected to happen, happened. I had a full body orgasm; but with no erection or ejaculation. That was the first time I ever experienced an orgasm without any sexual associations whatsoever. Sexual energy is so much more than just "sexual" as I came to find out. The entire experience lasted about two or three minutes and then it was over. I felt normal and went straight to sleep. When I woke up, however, I felt different; altered somehow, like my very genetic code was being transmuted to a higher level by some unseen force.

Roy Eugene Davis and the Center for Spiritual Awareness (I am a minister of CSA) do not promote or condone Kundalini Yoga. This is because people sometimes become confused and use Kundalini Yoga techniques to "get high" or alter Consciousness and they can become addicted to the states cultivated through the practices. One should use yoga, pranayama, and chanting to calm the body and mind so that they can see their true nature. One should not use these practices to "get a buzz" or "get blissed out."

After asana and as preparation for meditation, I recommend a round or two of breath of fire, a rapid expulsion of energetic toxins from the body. Then one may move on to alternate nostril breath to balance the hemispheres of the brain and also the Ida and Pingala nadis that run alongside the Sushumna nadi. And then finally one may practice Kriya Pranayama if they have been initiated by a qualified teacher in that tradition, or otherwise one may practice a simpler form of this pranayama known as Sushumna Breath; this is the process of moving prana up and down the sushumna nadi. I dare not describe any of these procedures in any detail, as pranayama is powerful and transformative and should be learned in person from a knowledgeable teacher who in turn learned from a knowledgeable teacher and so on.

Pranayama may be practiced for five to fifteen minutes or so as preparation for mediation practice. The practitioner should be in an environment free from any air toxins as they practice pranayama. Once the energetic body is calm and balanced, it is much easier to flow into meditation. If the energetic body is out of balance or erratic, one will find it difficult to meditate and impossible to experience superconsciousness. There is a reason Patanjali spelled out a specific order to the practice of Yoga in the eight limbs found in the Sutras. We work our way through each layer one at a time relaxing and harmonizing every sheath until we enter into Oneness.

Our autonomic nervous system, which is responsible for the "fight or flight" phenomenon, is greatly affected by a consistent pranayama practice. The autonomic nervous system is made up of two parts; the sympathetic and parasympathetic. The sympathetic gets us energized and ready to confront challenges and stressful situations. The parasympathetic de-energizes the body and is the originator of the relaxation response. Needless to say, in our modern busy lives the sympathetic nervous system is completely overtaxed, while the parasympathetic remains severely under-stimulated. With a consistent, daily pranayama practice we can balance out the disharmonies in the nervous system as we stimulate the parasympathetic nervous system over and over again. Pranayama, according to many recent University studies, is the absolute best way to stimulate and nourish the parasympathetic nervous system. One can easily experiment on their own with pranayama and notice almost immediately a reduction in stress levels and an increase in levels of relaxation.

In order to balance and harmonize the energetic layer of our Being, it is essential to activate and stimulate the parasympathetic nervous system. Once our nervous system is relaxed our energetic body, which is inextricably linked to the physical nervous system, is able to balance and harmonize. Yoga, in a sense, is a very physiological process. That is why it is of the utmost importance to maintain a healthy and functional physical body, and to take special care of our nervous system in particular. Adopting an Ayurvedic and Yogic lifestyle and keeping the body temple clean is the foundation of the physiological process of Yoga. Without this foundation, it is impossible to construct the internal environment necessary to experience higher states of Consciousness.

It is important to have the body ready and prepared to handle higher states of Consciousness. This is the problem posed by the use of psychedelic substances to elicit higher states. Most people that use these substances have not prepared the body temple to handle Kundalini experiences and major shifts of consciousness. That is why many people that try these substances "freak out." The physiological process of Yoga is a much safer route to experiencing higher states of Consciousness, as the body temple is proactively prepared ahead of time to handle these higher states.

is

6 MANAMAYA KOSHA AND PRATYAHARA & DHARANA

The manamaya kosha is our mental sheath or mind. The mind is a tool to be used and nothing more, and yet we are constantly identified with its contents. We go through our lives believing that we are our memories, fears, thoughts, likes and dislikes, mental patterns, tendencies, etc... None of these things have any permanency. They are fleeting, here one moment and gone the next, and therefore have no lasting reality. We are not our memories, because they change. We are not our thoughts, because they change. We are not our mental patterns or subconscious tendencies, because they change. We are not our likes and dislikes, because they change. We are that which never changes; the eternal soul. At our core we are Infinite and never change. All change is an illusional reality, always in flux, while the core of our Being is forever unchanging. It is the highest Truth and the ultimate Reality.

However, just because the physical world is always changing and impermanent does not mean that is has no value or purpose. We are all here for a reason. We have the ability and freedom here to exist and express in every kosha, in every dimension. We have a specific role to fulfill in the world for God via the mind, body, and personality. The world, even with its changing, fleeting nature, is still to be valued and regarded as part and parcel of God and Consciousness in manifestation. Infinite Consciousness is the substratum of all of existence and all of creation manifests out of It. Every layer of the physical plane is a manifestation of the Divine and all part of the grand Divine plan vibrating at different frequencies and ought to be regarded with the highest reverence.

I experienced firsthand the Divine vibratory nature of all of creation one time during a two day chanting workshop with a Brahmin who was trained in the Sama Veda, which is the world's oldest extant song. It has been chanted by Brahmins in the same manner continuously for over three thousand years. It is by far the most powerful and transformative thing I have ever chanted. I am one of a few hundred Westerners who knows how to chant the Sama Veda, and for that I feel incredibly blessed and grateful.

We chanted for about twelve hours a day for two days straight learning from this man and being initiated into the secret tradition. About eight hours into the second day I began having visions as we chanted. I was able to "see" the sounds and vibrations of the Sanskrit syllables. They appeared before me in the room as beautiful waves of rainbow light and sacred geometric patterns of perfect symmetry and form. I had the realization that sound was everything and everything was sound. After a few minutes, I began to see everything and everyone around me turn into sound, but sound that could be "seen" with the third eye. The tables and walls began to turn into visible sound waves and I was able to experience the various frequencies of all of manifestation.

All of creation is God singing everything into existence in a Divine harmony of different pitches, tones, and vibrations that coalesce into the forms that we experience in normal Consciousness. The universe is a song. If we learn to listen hard enough, we can hear it. If we can understand everything as sound or vibration, then I believe our science will be forever changed as we move into unknown territory. Recently, there have been many breakthroughs using sound waves to levitate small objects. I believe in the next few years, sound wave technologies will change the way we think about the universe and our energetic and vibrational relationship to it. My experience lasted well into the night and I only felt "normal" again when I woke up the next day, but like all such experiences it left a lasting residue. I can still sense the vibratory sound-like nature of all of existence, and I tend to "see" things as different frequencies of sound existing on a spectrum of Divine harmony being sung by the Lord into manifestation.

One can easily begin to witness their thoughts by sitting still and detaching awareness from the contents of the mind coming into a reaction-less and vibration-less state of pure observation. We may then experience thoughts as "separate" from ourSelves. By detaching awareness and concern from the contents of the mind, we can begin to experience Witness Consciousness. This is the first step into a much, much bigger experience of the universe and Consciousness. It might be easy to detach from our thoughts momentarily to get a taste of the Witness, but for most of us the cultivation of Witness Consciousness requires diligent practice and a little technique.

In order to transcend the manamaya kosha, yogis have used for millennia the limbs of pratyahara and dharana. Pratyahara may be defined as the removal of senses and attention from externals. Dharana is the focused concentration of the mind. In order to transcend the mental layer, it is necessary to use both of these limbs.

Pratyahara is the bridge from the external practice of Yoga to the internal practice. The first four limbs of yama, niyama, asana, and pranayama are all considered the external practice of Yoga, while pratyahara leads us into our internal practice of dharana, dhyana, and Samadhi. By removing our awareness from the senses and sensory input, we are preparing to dive into the inward ocean, and we are readying ourselves to experience the deeper layers of our Being.

Pratyahara, as I understand it and teach it, is quite simple. All one needs to do is close their eyes and make sure they are in a completely silent environment. If incense or smells of any kind in the meditation space tend to bother the practitioner, then they should be removed. There should be as few distracting sensory inputs as possible when sitting to meditate.

It is helpful to have the eyes closed during pranayama as preparation for pratyahara and dharana. However, during pranayama the attention should be on the breath and energetic body, while during pratyahara the attention should be removed even from the breath. Pratyahara is simply the retirement of the senses. Once the senses have been subdued by closing the eyes, being in a quiet, sattvic environment, and removing awareness from all inputs, then one is ready to begin the practice of dharana.

Dharana is the focusing of the mind as preparation for meditation. The most efficient way of achieving focused attention is through the use of a mantra. Mantra has been used for thousands of years as a way to control the wandering mind and bring it into one pointedness. Even christian mystics and monks use repetitive prayers to focus their attention towards God. It is a universal technique available to us all, and its simplicity lends itself to practical application. I do not believe that Infinite Consciousness would make it difficult for us to experience It. We have been left with a simple tool that with proficient use can bring us into union with the Divine in Samadhi. The use of mantra or dharana is preparation for dhyana, or meditation, and ultimately for Samadhi.

There are other meditation traditions that do not use mantra and instead use a breath awareness technique or another technique. I have experimented with many different meditation techniques and I must say that the use of mantra or simply listening for the Om vibration, is the best technique for focusing attention and awareness and transcending the lower layers. The problem with breath awareness is that the practitioner is still aware of the physical sheath as they meditate. Mantra allows us to hover above the physical sheath as we access and transcend higher and higher mental layers through mantra moving us closer to our ultimate destination of Pure Consciousness.

If mantra is ineffective or not enjoyable for certain practitioners, then they may simply listen for the Om vibration. In the Yoga Sutras in verses 1:27-1:29, Patanjali states the following:

The manifesting symbol of God is Om. One should meditate on this word, contemplating and surrendering to it. Meditation on Om results in cosmic consciousness and the removal of all mental and physical obstacles to success on the spiritual path.

To use this technique it may be helpful to chant Om out loud a few times. Then one may begin to recite Om in their head to themselves. After mentally chanting Om for a few moments, one should stop and then simply begin to listen for subtle sound frequencies occurring around the head and in one's field of awareness. One should feel themselves dissolving in the Om vibration and know that the source of Om is God. Om is the vibration from which all of God's manifestation emanates.

Mantra is one of the keys that can open the door of deeper layers of Consciousness. However, there are those few great meditators who do not require any technique or key whatsoever and can simply "dive right in" so to speak. This is certainly the exception rather than the rule. Most of us need some sort of technique to get the mind settled, even if we only use it for a few minutes. Once the mind is settled and we are ready for meditation, then the technique is irrelevant. I have been around certain teachers that truly believe that their technique is the best or is the only way, but they forget that once one is meditating the technique no longer has importance. With that said, I am partial to mantra, but there are other techniques that people use and have success with. Within the tradition of Kriya Yoga, mantra is taught and it is believed that the use of Sanskrit mantras in particular has a cleansing and balancing effect on the manamaya kosha. After years of practicing a specific mantra now, I can personally attest to the benefit of using a Sanskrit mantra on the manamaya kosha. I would recommend receiving a mantra from a qualified teacher and not just choosing one to use at random. However, a general one that any practitioner may use to get started with is "So Hum."

To practice mantra meditation in the Kriya Yoga tradition, one simply says silently in their head to themselves the vibration "So" on the inhale, and then on the exhale one repeats the vibration "Hum." The practitioner repeats the vibration in their Consciousness over and over until the mind is settled and calm. Once the mind is calm, one may set the mantra aside and sit in the silence. However, if one begins to have thoughts again, they can pick the mantra back up and begin using it until it is again no longer necessary.

The use of mantra is an organic process and should never be forced. We use the mantra to settle the mind, and set is aside when we no longer need it, and maybe we pick it back up if we need it again for a few minutes, and so on and so forth. When a thought arises, we just ease our attention back to the mantra. We should not force the awareness back to the mantra, but use the gentlest act of will possible to refocus our attention. "So" on the inhale, "Hum" on the exhale; that's it. The practitioner should not worry about the literal meaning or translation of the words So and Hum. Instead, we ought to endeavor to "feel" the vibrations of the words, rather than attempting to grasp them intellectually.

Daily use of a Sanskrit mantra will over time leave our Consciousness cleansed and purified, and we can more easily delve into meditation and higher states of Being. Mantra may be likened to daily mental hygiene. We use a toothbrush to clean our teeth, and we use mantra every day in the same way to clean and polish the mind.

It is very important to be ever cognizant of what we allow into our minds via the senses. We may practice pratyahara and dharana during our normal day to day routine even when we are not sitting formally to meditate. In the practice of pratyahara, we can be mindful of what we allow our senses to see, taste, touch, hear, and smell. For instance, watching gruesome and violent horror movies is not a good way to practice pratyahara. By allowing ourselves to experience certain things through the faculty of sense, we are also allowing our minds and nervous systems and even our energetic selves to experience those things. Over stimulation of the senses by any means is antithetical to a serious Yoga practice.

We can practice dharana throughout our normal day by keeping our attention focused on the task at hand, rather than allowing our attention to wander to past experiences and future concerns. Remaining fully present in all that we do is the best way of practicing dharana in our day to day lives. ADD is a modern affliction affecting many children and adults alike. It is an obvious outcome of our sensory overload culture. The practices of pratyahara and dharana are more important now than ever with all that we take in on a daily basis. If we become serious about our Yoga practice, then sensory distractions like alcohol, drugs, television, video games, pornography, and the like begin to fall off our radar, as we begin to see the negative attributes of sensory overload on our lives. There is nothing wrong with an occasional indulgence into sensory pleasure, but becoming addicted to sensory pleasure can cause major obstacles on the Spiritual growth path. Likewise, sitting around feeling guilty for a rare indulgence is about as productive on the path as addiction.

Pratyahara and dharana allow us to transcend the mind by balancing and relaxing the manamaya kosha. The retirement of the senses and the focused attention of the mind are prerequisites for meditation, just as asana and pranayama are prerequisites for pratyahara and dharana. The process of Yoga is like walking up a Divine staircase taking one step at a time as we get closer and closer to Oneness. If we miss a step, then we have to start all over again and may never reach the top of the staircase and open the door to Heaven. Patanjali left us with an instruction manual for how to move through the layers of our Being, but we have to follow the order given in the manual. Once the mind has been harmonized through the use of mantra, we are ready to dive into meditation. Mantra is not meditation, but a precursor to meditation. Meditation happens when the mind is still and silent and the need for mantra no longer exists.

7 VIJNANAMAYA KOSHA AND DHYANA

The vijnanamaya kosha is the ego-sheath. Sometimes this kosha is also translated as the wisdom sheath. When I refer to ego here I am not referring to egotism, which is the idea that I am superior to someone else. I am referring to egoism, which is the idea that I am Christopher Sartain, this body-mind-personality composite. The vijnanamaya kosha gives us our sense of separateness and uniqueness, and also allows us the opportunity to transcend this sense of separateness via "wisdom", which is why it is sometimes referred to as the wisdom sheath. Without it, we would not have an individuality. We are all units of the One Infinite Consciousness so we are always at one with God, but at the same time, we are **units** of God so we have some individuality as well. Infinite Consciousness or God, or whatever we choose to call it, is the ocean and we are drops of water in the ocean carrying with us all the characteristics of the entire ocean while maintaining some sense of individuality at the same time.

In order to function here on planet Earth it is quite necessary for us to maintain our sense of individuality. However, during times of meditation we can let go of that individuality for a period and merge our awareness with all that is, was, and ever will be. Unless we are willing to let go of that sense of individuation and come to terms with our Oneness, we will never experience deep levels of Samadhi and Oneness Consciousness. It is the sense of separateness from God or Infinity that keeps our Consciousness trapped within the confines of this delusional sense of reality called maya. This can be one of the more difficult steps in the process of Yoga, but in the end the surrendering of our limited sense of self-identity can be the simplest step too. Asana, pranayama, pratyahara, and dharana allow us to steady and relax the lower layers as preparation for dhyana, or meditation. Dhyana is what we use to transcend and move past the vijnanamaya kohsa so that we may experience the bliss of the anandamaya kosha.

Most suffering occurs because we believe we are something that we are not. At my core, I am not Christopher Sartain, because at some point he will perish and my soul will be recycled back into another form. To overly identify with Christopher Sartain is to suffer. We cannot expect to achieve any degree of Spiritual freedom unless we are willing to let go of our limited sense of self-identity. This step is more important than all the asana and pranayama in the world. One may practice asana, pranayama, and mantra for years and never have any transformative experiences simply because they are so identified with their temporary characters and roles.

Dhyana is a thought free state that occurs as the mantra comes and goes, and is experienced most deeply when the mantra fades away entirely and the practitioner is "just there". This thought free state is not necessarily Samadhi, but can be mixed with the lower levels of Samadhi. This is where descriptions with words begin to become inadequate. It is quite difficult to put into words the moving in and out of mantra, meditation, and Samadhi. The steps of dharana, dhyana, and Samadhi all flow in and out of one another as one makes their way into pure Samadhi states. One may notice that they are ever so gently reciting their mantra one moment, in a thought free state of peace the next moment, and experiencing states of Oneness shortly thereafter, only to return back to their mantra when they have a thought a few moments later. This is the organic process of meditation. One should let it flow naturally without any desire to control the outcomes of meditation practice. The more we practice and the more we let the process occur naturally without letting our will get in the way, the easier it becomes to still the mind and experience deep states of superconscious awareness resulting ultimately in Oneness Consciousness.

When the practitioner reaches a thought free state of dhyana and the mind is at one pointed attention, they should allow the process to occur on its own. Often times, when someone experiences thought free states for the first time, it is rather uncomfortable and their mind finds many clever ways to trick them back into having streams of thoughts. If this occurs, we should gently return to our mantra until we have another thought free gap. It is important to relax into the thought free gaps and allow the mind to enjoy the deep rest. This is when the magic begins to occur, but we should not allow ourselves to become too excited at this point; for this is just the beginning.

Once we have quieted the mind through mantra and meditation, anything is possible. From here we have entered what modern physicists refer to as the vacuum state. In this state at the quantum level, anything is possible. This is where all possibilities are made manifest and if one feels so inclined, this is a good time to recite a few positive affirmations or visualize positive and beneficial situations and relationships that one would like to manifest in their lives. It is fine to do these types of things on occasion, but most of the time we should simply enjoy our time in the deep silence and remain there in preparation for Samadhi.

Meditation is the key for severing our identity with the ego or lower case s self and it allows for the opportunity to identify with a much larger sense of Self. Without dhyana or meditation we cannot transcend the ego layer of our Being. Letting go of our limited sense of self-identity is one of the most important steps on the path of Yoga, if not the most important. Without this sacrifice, we cannot go all the way.

The fear of death is the ultimate blockade barring our entrance into the gates of Heaven. The reason that many people who have been meditating for years and years have not experienced Samadhi has little to do with their technique and much to do with their attachment to the body-mind-personality composite. The fear of death is irrational. It is impossible for us to die. We are Infinite and always have been and always will be. The body is a Divine vehicle that we use for a short time, discard, and return to when we are ready to have more experiences in this plane. We should no more fear death than we should fear losing our current automobile and having to acquire another one. It is the same thing from the standpoint of Spirit. We are here for a little while to play a role for the Lord, burn off some karma, and have new experiences as we evolve Spiritually.

When we die, our astral body migrates with our Consciousness and resides in the astral plane for a while. When we are ready and are attracted to a new form, our Consciousness enters the form of a new physical body and the cycle begins anew. We need not fear the death of any physical form, as it is a mere energetic transition from one form to another and is as natural as any other process or cycle in nature. Energy can neither be created nor destroyed.

The reason most of us do not have memories of past lives is because our Consciousness is not completely clear, and to be honest it is also because memories are not really all that important. From a Spiritual standpoint, memories are mundane. They exist so that we may function in time and space here on planet Earth and maintain a sense of personality and individuality, but in the grand scheme of things, memories are not all that important. So the next time we find ourselves feeling down over a negative memory of a past event, we should remember that it is like a temporary file stored in our computer banks for later reference if we need to access it and nothing more. We should always remain objective and never let negative memories of the past affect our present state of Consciousness. It is helpful to remind ourselves that we are the Witness of the memories and not the memories themselves.

We use mantra or dharana to relax and balance the manamaya kosha as preparation for dhyana or meditation. Once the mind is in a relaxed thought free state, we are said to be practicing dhyana if there is such a thing. It's not so much a practice as it is a surrendering to the process of Yoga. We do not force meditation, but instead allow it to happen on its own. Once we reach a state of meditation, our physiology is programmed to do the rest for us. The program is ready to go as soon as we are ready to use it. When we surrender ourselves to the process, we allow the layers of our Being to do what they do naturally. Within our Being lies all the knowledge of the universe. When we begin to align ourselves with Oneness, our Being is programmed to operate in a certain fashion like a Divine machine. All we have to do is press the "on" button through meditation. God takes care of the rest...

8 ANANDAMAYA KOSHA AND SAMADHI

The anandamaya kosha is the bliss sheath. This is where we experience the ecstasy and bliss of Yogic practice. The bliss experienced here is beyond what one would normally consider to be bliss or joy. The anandamaya kosha is extremely light and there is almost no density in ananda. The bliss experienced at the level of ananda is entirely different that an emotional form of bliss experienced on an emotional level. Bliss at the level of ananda is the sweetest ecstasy one can possibly imagine and then some. If language proved inadequate in describing meditation, then it will surely fall short in describing bliss and/or Samadhi in this chapter.

Roy Eugene Davis has often stated in his books and lectures that one should go beyond the bliss and ecstasy "all the way" to Infinite Consciousness. It is easy for us to get caught up in the bliss of anandamaya kosha. Many yoga asana practitioners get a small taste of the bliss body when they are coming out of savasana and they cradle up in a fetal position on their sides for a few moments. Most Yoga teachers do not allow enough time here and have students sit up immediately after savasana. I like to allow a minute or more in the fetal position to absorb and assimilate the practice and energy that has been cultivated through the practice. After curling up in a fetal position, one is asked to sit up slowly and come into an upright seated position. There is a definitive energetic shift that occurs right at the moment of coming to seated. One may experience a few moments of bliss here and get a small taste of the bliss body or anandamaya kosha. Waves of pranic energy may flow through the body during this time and once the practitioner has experienced these waves of energy a few times, they begin to occur during the entire practice and not just at the end during the relaxation portion. I know of yogis that are so sensitive that they feel the bliss waves with every movement of their bodies throughout the entire day.

Bliss is nice, but in order to reach our ultimate destination of Samadhi and Oneness, we must release all attachment to experiences of bliss and ecstasy. Meditation or dhyana can lead us into experiences of bliss, but we must "use" Samadhi as the final step in the process of Yoga to transcend the bliss body. Once we have transcended the bliss body, we have reached the layerless layer so to speak. Samadhi exists outside the bounds of physical space-time. It is beyond words. The experience of Samadhi leads us ultimately into a state I can only describe as Oneness Consciousness.

We can experience lower levels of Samadhi or superconsciousness while we are practicing mantra and flowing in and out of thought free states, but the deeper levels of Samadhi are experienced in thought free states of full and complete one pointed attention and awareness. Samadhi is the bringing together of our attention and awareness with the essence of our Being, Pure Infinite Consciousness. One can begin to feel the subtle effects of Samadhi during a thought free state when they have a sense that they are other than their mind, body, or personality. Samadhi is the full expression of the Witness. In Samadhi we have a sense that we are Infinite. After a Samadhi experience we do not believe that we are Infinite, we **know** that we are. It erases all fear and all doubt. During Samadhi we experience ourselves as we truly are, eternal and boundless. Samadhi should not be confused, however, with Self-realization or enlightenment.

The repeated experience of Samadhi and Oneness over time

leaves a lasting imprint and residue within the practitioner that can lead to Self-realization. One Samadhi experience is usually not enough to arrive at full Self-realization. Enlightenment is just the natural unfoldment of innate Spiritual knowledge that occurs when one continually dives into the ocean of Samadhi. Many yogis make the mistake of assuming that they are enlightened because they have experienced Samadhi a time or two. One may even form a "Spiritual ego" around the knowledge that they have experienced Samadhi and others have not. What they do not realize is that there is no person or thing that experiences Samadhi really. Samadhi occurs when the experiencer vanishes and there is only Oneness.

Oneness Consciousness is experienced when Shiva and Shakti, Yin and Yang, sun and moon, male and female all come together and realize simultaneously their Oneness with each other. It is truly indescribable with words and our limited language, but needless to say it is the ultimate aim of the steps laid forth by Patanjali in the Yoga Sutras, and it is the ultimate purpose of balancing and harmonizing all five koshas. Although, it is not really conducive to Spiritual Awakening to think of Oneness as an aim or goal. Oneness just is, all the time, everywhere. There is only Oneness. At our core, we are all One, and we are all enlightened already. All is possible in this moment; in the Here and Now. There is no need to complicate matters any further. All is One. We are that Divine Love, that Divine Light, and that Divine Oneness right Here, right Now! Enjoy!

9 EXPERIENCES WITH A MASTER

It wasn't until I met my first real Spiritual Guru or teacher, Roy Eugene Davis, that I began to experience authentic Spiritual growth. I yearned for deeper Spiritual knowledge when I was in my late twenties and I asked the Universe to provide me with a teacher that could show the way to higher understanding. And the Universe, as it often does, provided.

I can still remember walking into a local metaphysical bookstore in Dahlonega, Georgia and looking at the bookshelf as I walked by and seeing Yoganandaji's eyes shining like diamonds on the cover of Autobiography of a Yogi. God spoke to me in a very subtle manner that I am only now able to understand fully and told me to pick the book up and buy it. I read the entire treatise in a week's time and it quickly catapulted its way to the top of my favorite books list.

I knew the minute I read the book that I had some profound connection with Yogananda and the Kriya Yoga practice. I marveled at the stories of mystical yogis and their supernatural abilities. I also reveled in the thought that I too could attain Samadhi experiences and achieve an enlightened state similar to the yogis mentioned in the text. Upon reading Autobiography I began to seek an enlightened Master who could guide me in the same way that Yogananda had guided his pupils. As fate would have it, the last remaining living Teacher-disciple of Yogananda happened to live an hour from my house in North Georgia.

Within weeks of finishing Autobiography of a Yogi and deciding that I needed a real Guru, I saw an ad in the local newspaper about a weekend retreat at a place called Center for Spiritual Awareness on Lake Rabun near Clayton, GA. I asked Carolina if she would like to attend the weekend meditation retreat being offered and she agreed. Carolina and I were both looking to go deeper with our mediation practice and Roy was just the person we needed to teach us.

The first time I entered the meditation hall at CSA, I was hit with a feeling of intense nostalgia and familiarity, like I had been in a similar place with a similar energy many times before. I took that as a positive sign that I was right where I needed to be. The meditation hall had a "juiciness" to it that is incredibly difficult to put into words. When Roy came in the room for the first meditation at the weekend retreat, I could feel his presence immediately. It was unlike any other presence I had experienced up to that point. It is difficult to describe, but everything around him softens and the air surrounding him is given an extra jolt of life force and vitality illuminating everything and everyone in his path. Even though my eyes were closed, and it was dark in the room because it was 7am, I could sense a subtle light or glow all around me. I felt calmer in his presence than I had ever felt before and I knew during that first meditation with him that we had found a teacher.

Roy leads a very simple meditation without much ceremony or ritual. He enters the room silently and lights a candle and a stick of incense, usually sandalwood. He has a seat on his "throne" as he jokingly calls it and tells the audience to "open your mind and being to the Infinite." Sometimes he will lead a few rounds of chanting Om Namah Shivaya or Sri Ram Jai Ram. He will then offer a simple technique or two and tell the practitioners to discard the technique when it is no longer needed and sit in the silence. At the end of the thirty or so minutes, Mr. Davis asks the meditators to visualize planet Earth with all its life forms and to wish for them their highest good. He then leads a chanting of Om and it is over. I have come to appreciate the simplicity of this meditation and I guide meditators in a similar manner.

I studied Eastern Religion in college at the University of Georgia, even though I ended up with a useless degree in Political Science, but I had enough classes to understand the basic tenets of the most popular Eastern Religious traditions. Prior to meeting Roy, or even taking my first Yoga class for that matter, I was already well versed in the literature of Buddhism, Taoism, and Hinduism. As a matter of fact, I have been reading Buddhist texts since I was fifteen years old. Needless to say, I'm all read up on Eastern thought so I was familiar with the idea of enlightenment and enlightened Masters like the Buddha, but up until I met Roy, the Masters were just stories in an old book. I didn't realize at the time that there were living, breathing, people that were "enlightened" living on planet Earth right now! Seeing the Divine manifest in the flesh so to speak was one of the most singular important moments of my life. Anyone who has ever sat with Roy and resonated with his vibration knows exactly what I'm describing.

The rest of our first weekend retreat was spent in meditation and touring the grounds of CSA. Roy's library is impressive and is a treasure trove of rare Spiritual and mystical texts. I have spent hours in there perusing his collection and storehouse of knowledge. There is also small temple there called the Temple of all Faiths that has stained glass windows representing all the major world religions. I have experienced many deep meditations in all the different buildings I've visited during my retreats at CSA. The entire place is permeated with the grace of the Kriya Yoga Guru lineage and one of its current Teacher-successors, Roy Eugene Davis.

I was in a state of bliss upon leaving CSA after our first visit. I couldn't believe how automatic my mediations seemed around Roy. I couldn't ascertain at the time how a person's presence could alter my state of consciousness. It blew my mind that just being around someone could shift me into higher states of existence and Being. I was only to find out later that I was able to have these experiences most likely because of Roy's Shakti, a Divine and healing energy. Mediating with Roy was like diving in the ocean, whereas meditating at home alone during this early stage was like diving into a bathtub. Prior to my experiences meditating in front of Roy, the only other thing that had been able to raise my consciousness like that was psychedelic drugs. My interest in Yoga took on a whole new meaning once I realized that I could essentially get "higher", or raise my consciousness without the use of mind-altering substances.

I bought just about every book Roy has ever written in the next few months following our first meeting with him. I devoured as much of his writings as I could get my hands on and I practiced the Kriya Yoga meditation techniques set forth in his books, although I would have to wait an entire year after our first meeting to be initiated into the powerful and transformative Kriya Pranayama technique for which Kriya Yoga is primarily known. Even though I was still teaching public school at the time, I learned to have discipline with my meditations. I woke up at around 6am every morning so I could "spend my thirty minutes with God" as Roy likes to say.

This morning routine, initiated by Roy's teachings, has come to be something that I genuinely look forward to doing each and every day. The duration of the mediation and the exact details and sequence of my general morning routine has shifted over the years, but it started out with the basic mediation techniques set forth in the Kriya Yoga tradition, and these are still the basic techniques that I teach new meditators.

The techniques I used most often at the time were mantra, breath awareness, and listening for the Om vibration. At first, I didn't have much success and could never duplicate the mediations I was having when I would go visit Roy at CSA. I was patient even though mediation was quite painful at times in the beginning. Something inside me yearned for deeper and deeper mediations and I persisted with the techniques painstakingly each morning before a long stressful day teaching middle-schoolers.

About two months after our first retreat with Roy, we decided to go to another one. At this point, I had established an email correspondence with Roy asking him simple questions about the Spiritual path. In one of my emails I asked him if it would be alright to meet privately with him at the upcoming retreat, and to my surprise he agreed! When I got his reply, I can remember wanting to have a panic attack. What business did I have meeting privately with an "enlightened Master"? Who was I anyway? What kinds of questions does one ask an enlightened person after all? Now that I had my opportunity, I had no idea what I would talk about with Roy. To be perfectly honest, I really just wanted to be in his presence to imbibe some more of his Shakti.

Following an early meditation in the meditation hall, Roy sat down with me and asked me, "What can I do for you?"

As soon as we began our conversation he looked at the prayer beads on my wrist and grabbed them and popped them with the elastic against my wrist and gave me a little smirk...I responded by saying something really stupid like, "they're for mindfulness..."

We started off talking about what I do and where I live. I told him I lived in Dahlonega and that both my wife and I were school teachers. I told him that I taught middle school gifted students at the time. He asked about Dahlonega, and I told him it was the site of the first major gold rush in the US and then he remembered going through there about twenty years prior. He asked how I heard about the Center and I told him via an ad in a local Magazine for the International Kriya Yoga Congress and that after seeing the ad I began researching about him. I found out about the Center and the June retreat so I decided to go. He said that he didn't advertise locally much, but usually in national publications. He said just in the past few years, some local folks had started coming to the retreats and that he had the support of the local government, neighbors, and some of the churches.

He asked me if I was a regular meditator and I told him that I had been practicing a little since I was young, but that I had been introduced to Eastern religions for the first time in high school via the writings of the Transcendentalists like Emerson and Thoreau. He said he found out about them in the same way (in high school, but that he didn't learn they were involved with Eastern religions until later) and that they were reading the <u>Bhagavad Gita</u> and other Indian texts and that they helped introduce Eastern thought to the United States.

I told him that I had been side-tracked several times and that I had not always stuck to the path, but that I was beginning to experience some positive results with meditation. When I told him I had veered off the path to impress girls, fit in, and accumulate things, he said that was ok. He wanted to know what he could do for me. I told him that I was resolved to continue on the path and that I really wanted to know what the next step was.

He said, "Just keep going, stay out of trouble, keep meditating, eat a healthy diet, get plenty of exercise, and be nice to people."

I told him of my idea to start a meditation retreat in Chile with my wife in the next couple of years and he said that if I was leaving so soon then, "We have a lot of work to do."

He thought that the meditation retreat center in Chile sounded like a good idea and wanted to know more about that. He said that we didn't have to come during a retreat and that we could come any time for a private retreat as long as we called the office first and made arrangements. He said he would like to talk more often with me and meet more often. After the meeting, he stood up to leave and I told him we were going to see some waterfalls and he said that they would look really nice with the two inches of rain we had just received.

I felt a complete sense of peace when I was in his presence. He was very inviting, and welcoming and I never felt awkward or like I was wasting his time. Roy has always been sincere and honest in his interactions with me. Anytime I have a question, no matter how seemingly mundane, he offers a genuine, heartfelt, patient response.

After our first meeting, I was energized and inspired! I began meditating more consistently and reading almost non-stop, even during the day at my middle-school teaching job. It got to the point where sometimes I would just hand out busy work for my students to do just so I could sit and read Roy's books.

I began to correspond with Roy more and more and I became dedicated to the Kriya Yoga path and its lineage of Gurus. Kriya Yoga is an ancient Yoga path stemming from the Himalayas. Its founder, Mahavatar Babaji, was a mystical Christ-like figure who lived in a cave deep in the Himalayas. It is said that he is a Great Avatar and can manifest a physical body at will. Christ, the Buddha, Mahavir, and others have been considered Great Avatars in the Indian tradition. This embrace of multiple Masters is one of the characteristics of Vedanta and Yoga philosophy that I've really come to respect.

I grew up attending a very conservative Southern Baptist Church three times a week for the majority of my childhood. Needless to say, I received the typical brainwashing and indoctrination that the majority of American kids receive in their Judeo-Christian churches. You know...the good guy, the bad guy, the good place, the bad place, sex is evil, the planet is 10,000 yrs. old, the Bible is the only truth, enlightenment was only possible for Jesus and not any of us, reincarnation does not exist, all people on Earth who are not Southern Baptists burn in hell for all of eternity...good stuff! So when I discovered the Enlightenment traditions of the East when I was fifteen things began to change. I stopped attending my parents' church about the same time and began reading everything I could find on Buddhism, Taoism, and anything to do with Spiritual enlightenment.

Mahavatar Babaji was discovered one day by his most prominent disciple Lahiri Mahasaya while hiking around in the mountains during a business trip. Lahiri realized that Babaji was his Guru and he stayed and studied with him for a very short time and returned to his life as usual. Babaji instructed Lahiri to teach people the Kriya Yoga techniques that he had been taught, and to initiate others to do the same. Lahiri did so and attracted many new disciples, one of which was Sri Yukteswar, who would become Yogananda's Guru. Most people come to know Kriya Yoga from Yogananda's writings. His most famous work is still his <u>Autobiography of a Yogi</u>. Yogananda is almost single handedly responsible for bringing Yoga to the West. Without his Divine influence it may have taken many more years for Yoga to blossom in America.

The ancient Kriya Yoga techniques, revived by Babaji, include pranayamas, meditation techniques, and a few other kriyas, or actions. These techniques are ancient and have been practiced for thousands of years, but were reintroduced by Babaji. Kriya Yoga is a science in the sense that one is free to experiment with the techniques and decide for themselves its efficacy based upon their results. There are no tricks or scams. Try it...if it works, then keep doing it...it's so easy. Anyone who has diligently practiced Kriya Yoga for a few years can testify to its effectiveness.

You don't have to change your religion to practice Kriya Yoga or any Yoga for that matter. Just add the techniques to whatever you're already doing and you will soon become a better Jew or Christian or

Muslim or Jain or whatever. Yoga is a science, not a religion. It is a practice that can be added to any religion so that the religious practitioner can elicit the same religious experiences that are spoken of in their Holy scriptures, rather than merely worshipping others who have had religious experiences!

This is what Yoga promises...religious experience! I can remember being a young boy sitting in the pews yearning for a religious experience and realizing that it was never going to happen sitting in a Southern Baptist church. I knew, as did Roy Eugene Davis, at a very early age that the theology and philosophy espoused by protestant ministers was misguided and misinformed. I often wondered why we weren't able to experience what some of the saints and prophets had experienced in the past.

Roy also looked beyond fundamental Christian ideas when he was very young. When he was a teenager he began reading books on Yoga and Eastern philosophy just as I had. He read Yogananda's Autobiography when he was eighteen years old and hitchhiked from Ohio out to California to meet his future Guru. He spent a few years learning directly from Yogananda until his passing in 1952. Roy then started his own ministry eventually ending up in the North Georgia Mountains at the Center for Spiritual Awareness, which just happened to be an hour drive from where I was living at the time I read <u>Autobiography of a Yogi</u> and was looking for someone to teach me meditation...hmmmm???

Roy has taught the fundamental principles of Kriya Yoga and meditation as taught by his Guru for the last sixty years. His dedication to the Awakening of mankind is an inspiration to all seekers on the path regardless of tradition or background. Roy is the very embodiment of what is spoken of in the ancient Yogic texts. One might not know by looking at him, in his typical rural southern garb, but Roy Eugene Davis is a true Yogi through and through. Roy said once in a lecture that I was attending that he when he was growing up and beginning to learn about enlightened Masters that he did not care if any of them had actually ever been enlightened. He said, "I was going to do it anyway." That is the type of confidence that Roy conveys. He did not care if there had never been an enlightened person in history, he was "going to do it." From an early age, Roy knew that he would be Spiritually enlightened and that he would travel the world teaching the path to God, and that is what he has done in dedicated fashion nearly his entire life.

I cannot express how fortunate and blessed I feel to have studied under Roy for these years. It was my introduction to real Spirituality and meditation. Roy exemplifies the role of householder. In many Eastern traditions, it is said that there are only two Spiritual paths; renunciate and householder. You're either a monk or you're married with children. I am married and am therefore a householder like Roy. He gave me a role model to follow. It is still hard for me to fathom how an "enlightened Master" can be married and lead a normal life. He's managed to do it successfully for decades and has never looked back. Roy is easily able to balance superconscious states with everyday living.

My "training" under Roy was completely informal. I went to approximately twenty retreats in the span of about five years and Carolina and I stayed at CSA several times to meet privately with Roy even when there were no scheduled retreats. We even had the opportunity to teach asana practice at a couple of retreats for Roy.

After a year of practicing Kriya Pranayama and the other techniques set forth in the Kriya Yoga system, I began to have deeper meditations. I began to feel as though my body were made entirely of Light and there was a sense that my brain was being cleansed by the hands of God, and I could perceive this happening as it was occurring. I could literally (and still can at times) feel my brain being rewired and reorganized while I meditated. Also, the more I practiced Kriya Pranayama, the more I began to feel my spine and the subtle energy channels that run along it. I also began noticing a distinct fluid being formed in the brain and dripping down into my mouth. This is the real "Soma" or nectar that is spoken of in the esoteric Yogic texts.

Roy introduced me to the "real Yoga". Prior to reading Autobiography of a Yogi and meeting Roy, all I knew of Yoga was asana. I didn't know that meditation, pranayama, lifestyle, etc. were all terms that fell under the larger umbrella term Yoga. I really thought Yoga meant asana alone. It's truly amazing how utterly uneducated most Yoga practitioners are in the U.S. about the true history of Yoga and the real meaning of the term itself. Indeed, most Yoga instructors in this country are equally as uninformed as their students about the true nature of this ancient practice, which involved little asana in ancient times. The suppression of the Sacred Science of Yoga by the Christian West is unfortunate, but that suppression has nearly run its course as Truth can only be hidden by the darkness for so long before the Light begins to pierce the veil of ignorance. Even in the Yoga Alliance Standards (YA certifies Yoga Instructors) one is now required to teach Yoga Philosophy, including the eight limbs according to Patanjali.

My wife and I were ordained teachers/ministers in the Kriya Yoga tradition on July 5th, 2012. It was decided that when we moved to Colorado that we would establish a small CSA meditation group in Crestone and so Roy ordained us both impromptu just as he had been ordained by his Guru some sixty years earlier. I cannot express just how fortunate my wife and I both are to be a part of this Spiritual lineage and to have the opportunity to learn from a direct disciple of Paramahansa Yogananda.

There is no need for the deification and worship of the Guru in a balanced Yoga practice. It is important for us to remember that even the Masters are human. There is nothing wrong with showing devotion towards one's teacher, but this should be practiced within reason. Personality cults based around the worship of only one teacher have run their course. The message is far more important than the messenger and it is important for any Yoga practitioner to keep that in mind.

According to Mr. Davis, Yogananda would often times remind his devotees that, "God is the real Guru," and that he was just God's messenger. To be honest, I have been in the presence of many powerful teachers, but I have always maintained a sense of dispassionate objectivity towards my teachers so that I can learn from them unfettered. I love Roy Eugene Davis with all my heart, but I also understand that he is not to be worshipped, nor does he wish to be. Roy understands the Guru-disciple relationship better than anyone, and he has managed to quietly mentor many fine teachers and ministers throughout the last sixty years without much fanfare, glitz, or glamour. He has a style all his own that I find to be authentic and endearing. Anyone who has had the great privilege to study with him should consider themselves truly blessed.

10 ECSTATIC POEMS

"Hope"

The bliss of meditation gives me hope

The DIVINE spark that lies within

Severing ties to this robotic entrapment

From the outside looking in

I see my little ego, full of fear and uncertainty

I take pity on it, and allow it to be

"Merge"

I interweave my fate with yours

My karma becomes your karma to extinguish in the flames of

DIVINITY

Surrender of the ego

Anguish and despair due to worldly attachment evaporate like drops

of morning dew rising heaven-bound to merge with the clouds of

your unconditional LOVE

Your GRACE never ending

Devouring my desires, emotions, and memories like a starving beast

Acceptance of the change you affect in my life

No resistance to GOD's will

GOD's intermediary - acting on HIS behalf

Yearning for freedom from this bondage of ignorance

My soul awakening like a paralyzed patient from a coma

So many lives lived to arrive here

Bonds unbroken in this Earth plane

INFINITY awaits!

"Glue"

Paralyzing desires -- stuck to this world

The glue that binds me here...

I manage to peel away some glue, but still a residue remains

I use my meditation razor blade and scrape the residue daily

In doing so, I dull my blade

I sharpen it with devotion

God give me the strength to keep my blade sharp

and to realize the glue is fleeting

Make my astral body as fine as polished steel

so that nothing may adhere to it except your Light

If my soul should return to this adhesive planet

allow me to walk freely with razor blade shoes

"Drop"

Rain drops fall down and merge with Mother Earth

only to evaporate and return to the sky

A never ending cycle...water makes no choice

Lord, make me as pure as the rain drop

so that I may come and go without suffering

"Shadow"

The greater the Light of God that shineth upon me

the more evident my shadow becomes

My darkness...my greatest Teacher

"Leaves of Karma"

The autumn of my life has begun

I feel my old form dying

Each karmic leaf turning brown

Preparing for its final descent

Mother Earth patiently awaiting its arrival

The wind, temperature, and rainfall of my life

creating proper circumstance for each leaf to fall

One cannot force such things

Every karmic leaf will fall on its own time

"Holy Garbage Man"

It seems a selfish thing to do Lord

to give my poisonous karma to you

In your wholeness you have become a Divine receptacle

The toxic waste dump for my cosmic sludge

My filth continued to pile up...trashcan overflowing

Until you, the Holy Garbage Man

came to free me of my wasteful collection

Some day my entire heap will be burned

in your vast incinerator of INFINITE LOVE!

"Abyss"

Waking up is the same as being asleep

The difference is an abomination

The self is immaterial

Floating with the current

The texture is but a vibration

Curling endlessly through the yugas

Time immemorial lasting nevermore

An illusion of smoke and mirrors

Empty of depth

Deep beyond meaning

Terrible storms beyond the mind

Rage without contemplation

Tangled web of existence

In and out of the void

What universe is this?

I've landed on no foundation

The lips of Mother Earth kiss me

Lifted up beyond the horizon

The sky is no more

Past and future meet

And explode into nothing

Activity ceases

The mists of lore retreating

The grains of sand receding

Into space not withstanding

A chemical reaction

Forcing into being

That which cannot exist

Somber morning reminder

Of what used to be

Shall be no more

Everlasting warmth

Touching not my face

But absorbing my essence

An ephemeral illusion

The bitter taste of knowledge

The burden of consciousness

The mystery of moment

Awake is no different

Than the rock I stand upon

"Aloft"

Aloft in solitude

I fear no reminder

Of times forgotten

Past lives remembered

Do not hurry

There is no meaning in haste

Who are you racing?

When do you know you've won?

How can you tell?

The race never was

A trick of the void

Illusion draws you in

You draw in the illusion

You perpetuate its existence

You ponder its importance

Leave it to the gods

Stand alone in your place

Make no big waves

Drop your defenses

There is no offense

Lower your shields

The arrows are nothing

Your mind awaits

Arrival of senses

Devoid of meaning

Lost in the muck

Of time everlasting

Of space interdependent

Of things impermanent

Fleeting in the moment

The solitude of sunshine

The masks of interaction

Coming off in the shade

Eternal flames of mountains

Shining through to the shadows

Illuminating the field

With overtones of abundance

Dancing with fate

Playing with madness

Falling for the game

Stellar views renew me

In pastures made of green

Touching my feet

ABOUT THE AUTHOR

Chris Sartain has been practicing Yoga for over twelve years and has now taught Yoga and Meditation for the last five years. He and his wife owned and operated a Yoga studio in Dahlonega, GA and were part of a thriving Yoga movement in the North Georgia Mountain Region. Chris received his Yoga Alliance Teaching Certification through Peachtree Yoga Center in Atlanta, GA and his Ayurveda Certificate through the American Institute of Vedic Studies in Santa Fe, NM. He also studied meditation and learned the ancient techniques of Kriya Yoga with Roy Eugene Davis, a living direct disciple of Yogananda. Chris was ordained a teacher/minister in the tradition by Mr. Davis in July 2012. Chris currently leads Yoga Alliance Teacher Trainings and teaches weekly Yoga and Meditation classes in Crestone, Colorado where he and his wife now live. Chris has a Bachelor's degree in Political Science from the University of Georgia and a Master's degree in Education.

Christopher Sartain

RECOMMENDED READING

The Holy Science, Swami Sri Yukteswar

Autobiography of a Yogi, Paramahansa Yogananda

Whispers from Eternity, Paramahansa Yogananda

A Master Guide to Meditation, Roy Eugene Davis

An Easy Guide to Ayurveda, Roy Eugene Davis

Paramahansa Yogananda as I Knew Him, Roy Eugene Davis

The Eternal Way, Roy Eugene Davis

The Science of Self-Realization, Roy Eugene Davis

Long Pilgrimage, John G. Bennett

Eastern Body Western Mind, Anodea Judith

Yoga for Your Type, Dr. David Frawley

The Yoga of Herbs, Dr. David Frawley

Made in the USA
Middletown, DE
29 June 2015